DISINHERITING
THE IRS

DISINHERITING THE IRS
Tips & Tactics to Stop Uncle Sam from Taking Your Legacy

Copyright © 2025 Stephen A. Bonfa
All rights reserved.

ISBN: 978-1-964046-64-8

Expert Press
www.ExpertPress.net

Editing by Tamma Ford
Copyediting by Wendy Lukasiewicz
Proofreading by Heather Dubnick
Text design and composition by Emily Fritz
Cover design by Casey Fritz

DISINHERITING
THE IRS

Tips & Tactics to Stop Uncle Sam from Taking Your Legacy

STEPHEN A. BONFA, ESQ

Master of Laws in Taxation

To Carmela, Anthony, and Isabella—

Whenever Uncle Sam tries to get their hands in my pockets, he always comes up short because you three were already in there—whether for ice cream, trips, singing lessons, electronics, or just because! If anyone's going to empty my pockets, it should be the people I love most.

With all my love
(and whatever's left in my wallet),
Stephen

CONTENTS

INTRODUCTION

He said that there was death and taxes, and taxes was worse, because at least death didn't happen to you every year.
—Terry Pratchett, *Reaper Man*

I wrote this book to do something tricky and make you think about what most of us prefer to ignore: planning for your death and thinking about taxes. But don't worry. It's not all doom and gloom. I intend to drop some important knowledge bombs on you and, best of all, get you motivated to take action. So, pour yourself a glass of your favorite beverage before we get started (coffee, tea, soda, or something stronger—no judgment here), grab your highlighter, and take a seat in your favorite but slightly uncomfortable chair. It's time to face the facts and start doing what you've been avoiding for far too long.

We will be talking about America's two most terrifying words.

Uncle. Sam.

Dealing with Uncle Sam, the IRS, and your state tax office—taxes in general—is scary to most of us. We would all like to disinherit our least favorite "uncle." It will be my pleasure to show you how to do just that, if not in entirety, in a number of advantageous ways.

We will also be talking about America's second most frightening topic.

Our own death.

Is this you in that picture? My goal is to help you lift your head out of the sand. We all know that education and knowledge are keys to letting go of fears, because after all, we fear what we don't understand.

I'm a lawyer and have earned the highest degree a lawyer can earn: the LLM—*Legum Magister* in Latin, or in my case, Master of Laws in Taxation. This is the post-graduate degree for attorneys and is the general equivalent of a PhD in the legal field. My advanced field of study is all about taxation and avoiding tax when you pass away. I pursued my LLM in Taxation focusing on estate planning because the US tax code is not a DIY affair.

Even for untrained lawyers, taxation is a daunting matter.

When I first started focusing my practice on estate planning back in 2004, I was out to help middle-class people with their last wills. I quickly learned that my estate plans, without knowing estate taxation, left the biggest blind spots in my client's plan. This was especially true for middle-class families (like my parents). Moreover, when I approached my colleagues for help and said, "I have a tax question," they immediately backed away and threw holy water at me before I could finish. All this to explain that, to make a complete estate plan, your planner needs to know and keep up with our country's constantly changing tax laws.

The primary areas in which I help clients in my law practice are estate planning, Medicaid, and elder law planning. In all those topics, taxation plays a big, big role. My education and experience allow me to discuss the tax implications in estate planning. The goal of this book is to educate you on how to keep more of your wealth in your family's pockets and to keep Uncle Sam's hands out of your family's pockets.

Uncle Sam has provided the guidebook for us taxpayers to pay only our fair share of taxes to him. We only need to know what's in the 6,871 pages of the US tax code and the over 75,000 pages in the US Treasury's official interpretation of the tax code. Today is the best time to start disinheriting that greedy uncle of ours.

To beat Uncle Sam, we need to plan, plan, and replan over and over again—and sometimes years in advance. Especially in today's chaotic political times, what worked three years ago may not work today.

Estate planning is for everyone, whether you have saved "just a little" money, invested in "just one little" asset, or if your last name is Zuckerberg or Bezos.

So sit back with that drink and come with me as I show you how to use the provisions of the tax code to your benefit. Let me give you the information you need so Uncle Sam won't take more than his fair share of your family's inheritance.

PART I

Why Your Inheritance Needs a Game Plan

*What's the difference between the tax code and
a rottweiler? A rottweiler lets go when you die.*
—Every tax professional in the United States

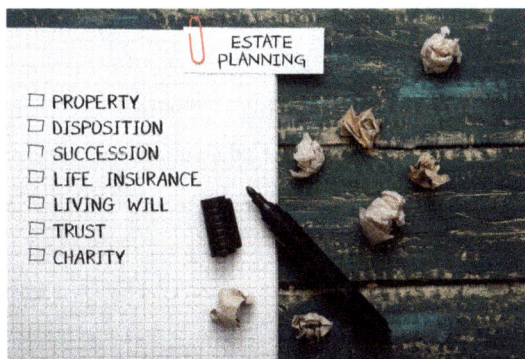

Estate planning is, first, a detailed look at your wealth and all
your assets during which you organize or reorganize them
in a tax-efficient manner. Tax efficiency means mitigating
(reducing) or eliminating taxes where legitimately allowed.

> **The best time to plant a tree was thirty years ago. The second-best time is today.**

Estate and tax planning can be started at any age, and the sooner the better. The best estate plans are created with lawyers who know your family and financial situation and can craft your plan to include financial, tax, family, and legal considerations. A well-developed estate plan should include several types of legally binding documents.

Experts should draft your plan to direct who gets your property and how it is to be distributed when you pass away, while paying keen attention to the tax ramifications to both your estate and your heirs who survive you.

Your plan's preparation should be made with an eye additionally focused on mitigating or eliminating inheritance (a.k.a. estate) taxes. This is where most individuals' eyes glaze over. I understand. Taxes are complex (so complex that I had to go back to law school for three more years to get my Master of Laws in Taxation). Even with Google searches and ChatGPT, the average American doesn't have a clear idea of how to "work the rules" to their benefit. This is where I come in.

Once I get an understanding of your particular family and financial situation, I can work within your goals to save you and your heirs lots of money. Without paying attention to the tax picture, however, you're giving Uncle Sam a free ticket to reach further into your pocket and grab more than he should.

A third aspect to estate planning makes many of my clients uncomfortable. It involves planning for the final period of their own life, should you be unable to attend to your own affairs for whatever reason.

Why should people be interested in preparing their estate plan? Why should people be focused on discussing and drafting a plan as early in life as they can?

Taxes.

Yes, taxes. Collecting that money from you is Uncle Sam's whole goal, and he's skilled at it. He's adept at taking more of a cut of your inheritance when you're gone than you legally and legitimately need to give him.

Do you really want Uncle Sam to be the primary beneficiary of your wealth when you pass away? Or would you rather have a say in who gets what, and how and when?

Plan!

This book will focus on avoiding, mitigating, reducing, and eliminating your potential estate tax liability.[1] It's all done through proper planning and properly documenting your wishes.

That's the big picture. Let's get into more detail now.

---

1   I am licensed and have worked in the state of New York. While comments regarding federal rules apply to us all, my examples throughout this book (unless otherwise noted) are based on New York law.

CHAPTER 1

Myths and Fears Around Estate Planning

We fear things in proportion
to our ignorance of them.
—Christian Nestell Bovee

There are misconceptions, myths, and lots of fears with regard to estate planning in general and wills and trusts specifically. My goal is to clear that up for you throughout these pages.

As most people know, in a fuzzy way, wills and trusts are among the primary (but not the only) useful documents in an estate plan. First, let's get clear on what exactly a will and a trust are.

Will

A last will and testament, or just a last will, is a legal document that provides instructions for how a person's assets and affairs should be handled after their death. Wills cover all assets that are in your name only.

A will takes effect after the person passes away, and it must go through probate, which is a public court process. The will thus becomes part of the public record and is available to anyone who wants to read it.

A will notably allows you to name guardians for minor children. It can be revised or changed during your lifetime.

Trust

A trust is a legal arrangement where a trustee manages assets for the benefit of designated beneficiaries. A trust only protects assets that have been transferred into (or are held within) it. A trust can take effect during your lifetime (living or inter vivos trust) or after death (testamentary trust).

Trusts avoid probate and thus keep your affairs private. Trusts allow for the management of assets if you become incapacitated, and they provide more control over how and when assets are distributed. A trust can be revocable (changeable) or irrevocable (no changes are possible or are difficult to effect). There are several types of irrevocable trusts, and I will discuss a fair number of them in the coming chapters.

It Is Never, Ever Too Early

The most startling myth—and real fear—I hear from people is that writing an estate plan will cause their death. I believe that this superstition arose from people waiting until they're facing their mortality and then, moments before the inevitable, are forced to make a plan. I promise you: Writing your estate will not kill you. Prepare your plan.

Sh*t Happens

Life throws you curve balls. A well-thought-out estate plan is important to have in more circumstances than you might now believe or imagine. And if you still need convincing, I have stories coming up that will change your mind.

Case in point: I had a twenty-three-year-old client with significant wealth. He acquired his money partially through an inheritance and partially because he was successful in the stock market. Unfortunately, he died in a personal injury accident. He was single and had no children.

He passed away without a will. No trust. No plan whatsoever. The money went to his parents according to the rules of intestate (which I will explain in a coming chapter), and it was *a lot* of money. The first tragedy was his untimely passing away. The second tragedy was that a significant portion of his inheritance was heavily taxed. The third tragedy was that when his parents inherited his assets, they were knocked off their needs-based health care.

At the time of his death, my client was caring for his parents who were both on government health care assistance for long-term care. The inheritance caused his parents to become ineligible for their government assistance. They had to use their son's inheritance to start paying for their care individually and change their medical providers.

If the young man had had the forethought to say to himself, "My parents are on assistance, what happens to them if something happens to me? Is there something I can do now? Let me talk to Stephen and see what I can do," he could have done some proper planning to allow his parents to remain on assistance and keep his legacy out of Uncle Sam's hands.

While I was able to assist his parents to some degree after the fact, the young man's parents had their lives uprooted in more ways than just emotional. You don't want that to happen to your loved ones. It is never, ever too early to plan.

If you're young, the flip side of that coin is that you may not think you have enough money yet to do such planning. You're struggling to care for disabled elders or a disabled child with the money you're earning—or to meet the mortgage every month. You don't have the mental bandwidth to set about planning.

Remember that estate planning when you're a parent is yet another way to take care of your children—and like for our twenty-three-year-old, it is also a way to care, perhaps, for your parents.

Seek Professional Guidance

People also mistakenly believe in the all-American DIY and that it's always a great way to go. They believe that if they download a template will off the internet and fill it out, it will be enough to protect their assets and avoid probate. They believe that it will be a complete plan.

In my experience, template wills fail you on several levels.

A general all-encompassing general template isn't a good way to handle your affairs. If you want to avoid inheritance tax, if you have assets in several states, or you have specific circumstances that require special planning (like elderly parents or a disabled child to care for), you need a professionally drafted estate plan valid in your state of residence.

I've had clients come to me to review their template wills, and they usually walk away with me having to redo everything. They didn't understand that the boilerplate words written in legalese meant the opposite of their wishes. The template will was not state-specific. Every state has its own rules and regulations, and often its own required forms.

Aside from what is in the template will, clients attempting a DIY will fail to take the steps that make it a valid will in their state. Some states don't require witnesses, others require two witnesses, yet others require three witnesses.

Moreover, you have to go through the execution formalities of your particular state and say the magic validating words at signing for your will to be upheld in court. In some states, you can write a will, sign it, and have it notarized—that's it for the will to be valid. In New York State, that is not valid. Two people need to witness the signing, and the formalities of the signing are specific and technical.

Sure, take notes to get your thoughts together and be inspired by some internet list to do so. But always let an attorney draft your will. Have the attorney explain the various legal terms, explore your specific needs and goals, and take the correct steps to execute your plan so that what you want to happen, actually happens.

"

Where there's a will, there's a relative.
—Ricky Gervais

Note that even with a will or a revocable trust, you haven't protected all your assets. Sorry. I often talk to clients who believe that if they create a revocable trust, they have protected their assets from Medicaid and other creditors (more on that later). Again, not so. It has to be a particular type of trust and, in this case, a specific type of irrevocable trust.

Here's one more big misconception to chew on. "Stephen, you're saying I need a will *and* a trust? I don't have enough wealth to worry about." Wrong. Estate planning with both a will and one or more trusts isn't just for the wealthy among us.

Are you starting to see how much you need an attorney's guidance?

Get Your Thoughts Together

What can you do before consulting me? Get your thoughts together about your assets and your wishes. Take a piece of paper and start brainstorming:

- List all the assets you have without worrying right now about how much they're worth or if they qualify as wealth.
- Write all the names of who you want your assets to go to.
- Note any special circumstances of your beneficiaries.
- And then come see me with that write-up.

I will create your plan with your goals and situation in mind. I can do this because I ask you questions about things you haven't considered or may not even know you need to consider in the first place (hint: taxes).

I have to say it straight up: With a Master of Laws in Taxation, and as an elder law and estate attorney, too, I know things about the US tax code that I'm sure the IRS would not like to have broadcast. That's because I know how to manipulate the tax code to your benefit. Understanding the tax code isn't an exercise for the faint of heart, believe me, so consult me.

Throw all your objections to estate planning out the window. Swallow that urge to procrastinate. Make no more excuses. Move forward by engaging with an experienced estate planning attorney. Do this now while you have control over who gets your stuff, how they get it, and when.

CHAPTER 2

The Purpose of an Estate Plan

A good plan is like a road map: It shows the final destination and usually the best way to get there.
—H. Stanley Judd

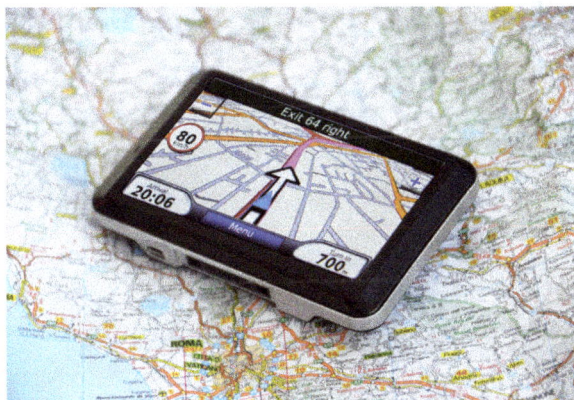

The most basic definition of an "estate" is the "total of all property, assets, and legal rights owned by an individual, especially at the time of their death, and regardless of its value or size." I work with clients to protect their legacy and preserve their wealth. I can work with you to eliminate the distress and stress among your heirs and beneficiaries by creating a well-thought-out, correctly drafted estate plan.

My professional philosophy is not to tell you *what* to do but *how* to accomplish your goals. You're the driver, and I'm your GPS navigator giving you several route options and navigating the best path to your destination.

Great estate planners put things together only after conversations with you, after educating you, and once they understand your family dynamics and all your assets. They put it together in a set of legally binding written documents called your "estate plan." The documents, taken together, state where, to whom, and how you wish your property and possessions to be distributed after you pass away.

What goes into an estate plan? I like to say there are three buckets of planning:

1. The who and what. A written plan ensures that your chosen heirs get what you intend them to get.

2. Long-term care asset protection. This planning protects your home and life savings from long-term health care costs.

3. Tax efficiency. An estate plan is asset organization, reorganization, and protection planning for estate tax reduction or elimination. This plan is devised to benefit you during your lifetime and benefit

your heirs after your death (in other words, you disinherit Uncle Sam to the degree allowed by the US tax code).

There are other purposes that might apply more individually depending on your circumstances, and I'll be addressing a number of those circumstances in these pages. These, however, are the big three.

Reading this book will not only educate you but also inspire you to act and address the areas of your life and legacy that need attention. Next, you call me to discuss your goals, needs, and circumstances. Planning today means you can make clear, informed decisions now, as opposed to the government and the courts making the decisions for you and your beneficiaries later. You don't want the courts involved if you can avoid it. Planning now helps you avoid it.

About Those Taxes

Individuals and families want to protect their inheritance, and well they should. They want to and should disinherit Uncle Sam to the degree legally possible, and it is entirely ethical to do so. The more you keep, the more you get to spend in your lifetime, and the more you get to give to your family when you're gone.

CHAPTER 3

No Plan Is a Plan, and It Is the Worst One Possible

No estate plan? Get ready for unnecessary costs, stress, and the government making decisions about your family's inheritance according to their best interests.
—Stephen Bonfa

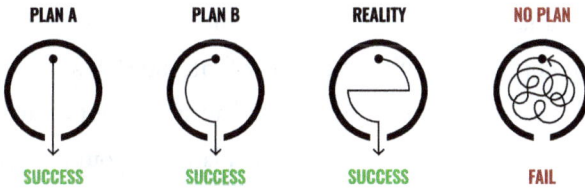

PLAN A	PLAN B	REALITY	NO PLAN
SUCCESS	SUCCESS	SUCCESS	FAIL

To summarize the woeful state of preparation for America as a whole: Two-thirds of US adults have no will or other estate planning in place,[2] with serious implications for grieving family members and heirs looking to settle the deceased's affairs. There is always uncertainty about what the courts

---

2   "How Many Americans Have a Will?" Gallup, June 23, 2021, https://news.gallup.com/poll/351500/how-many-americans-have-will.aspx.

will do in the absence of an estate plan. And differing state laws, differing goals among potential heirs, family addiction issues, and minor child guardianship concerns are just some of the complicating factors when you pass away without a plan.[3]

What About in New York State?

If you don't have an estate plan, the New York State government is the legal authority that directs what happens to your possessions. It will name guardians to your children and determine how your inheritance is taxed. You don't want to leave your family and loved ones in that situation.

This isn't just the case in the state of New York. If you don't have an estate plan—a will, a trust, or some other legally drafted instrument that dictates what happens to your assets when you pass—every state and the District of Columbia have laws of "intestate succession." This default rule is commonly called the "laws of intestate" (laws governing the estates of those who "passed away without a will"). If you haven't created your own estate plan with your particular interests in mind, don't worry—the government will do it for you. You can trust the government to do so with your and your family's best interests in mind. And I also have a bridge to sell you real cheap.

---

3   Deborah Nason, "'Your Loved Ones Will Already Be in a State of Trauma.' The Ramifications of Dying Without a Will," *CNBC*, October 29, 2022, https://www.cnbc .com/2022/10/29/here-are-the-legal-and-personal-ramifications-of-dying-without-a-will.html.

Without an estate plan, it is the government that dictates what happens to your inheritance according to their goals, not yours.

Think about it. You may have had particular ideas on who gets your house, who gets your other pieces of property, who gets your checking account, who gets whatever specific treasure of yours. You may even have told George, your best friend Serena, or your cousin Tony that they can have your stamp collection, your comic book collection, or that watch that passed from great-granddad to grandad to father to you in every war since World War I.

Here's the rub: Saying it with your hand on your heart and in front of one hundred witnesses won't make it so. You need to have a validly drawn-up and executed estate plan that ensures that George, Serena, and Tony get what you told them they would get—because you state it in writing to be so.

If you don't make that plan, your possessions might end up with individuals you don't want to get them. Families don't always live in peace and harmony. Sometimes there are bad apples on the family tree. Without a plan, those bad apples might get your prized Harley, even if you would never have given it to them. If you don't designate who gets it in your estate plan, that bad apple might walk away with the entire tree.

If you have minor children, you need a plan. You don't have a crystal ball that says, "I will live to raise my kids and see them married with children." If you disagree on every point of child-rearing with your only sister, you don't want her to be the one raising your children in the case of your early demise. Dying intestate means the courts can decide that your sister gets your children.

If you pass without an estate plan in New York, the disposition or distribution of your wealth and assets is in the court's hands. That's the bottom line. If you were waiting around to plan, think about those aspects of the issue. Plan now.

Who Gets What

If you pass intestate, and you're married and don't have children, according to the laws of the state,[4] your spouse gets 100 percent of your assets. If you're married and have children when you pass, your spouse doesn't get 100 percent, nor do your children get 100 percent. In New York, the first $50,000 goes to your spouse and then one-half of the remainder goes to your spouse and the remaining half goes to your children equally.

I'll bet your spouse didn't see that one coming.

The state will keep going up, down, forward, and backward through your family tree to find heirs. If none are found after searching several generations, the government takes your assets for itself.

Allow me to hammer this point: It's important to know who you want and who you don't want to inherit, but

---

4   Note that not every state of the union recognizes common-law marriage. The definition of "spouse" and "marriage" differ from state to state. Inform yourself.

you also must document it in a will or other court-accepted types of documents. Do you really want New York State and the federal government to be the final recipients of your wealth?

Avoid this confusion. Plan now.

New York State Intestate Distribution

Surviving spouse with no children:
- All to spouse

Surviving spouse and surviving children:
- Spouse gets first $50,000, then the spouse gets 50 percent and children split the other 50 percent

No spouse but surviving children:
- To decedent's issue

No spouse or surviving children:
- All to decedent's parents equally

No surviving parents:
- To decedent's siblings or nieces/nephews

No surviving siblings or nieces/nephews:
- To decedent's maternal and paternal grandparents

No surviving grandparents:
- To aunts and uncles or cousins

Eventually, the government takes it all.

When you have an estate plan, you're the decision-maker. Who gets what is your choice. There are three usual ways to distribute profit: per stirpes, by representation, and per capita. In a will or trust, you can state which manner you prefer.

Per stirpes. "Per stirpes," or "by branch," is the traditional way to pass property down, through family branches.

By representation. This method says everyone gets a share, but then it gets recombined per generation. Say you have three brothers with only one living, and from those brothers, you have one nephew from one brother and two nieces from the other. Here, the surviving brother will take one-third, but then the two-thirds will be recombined, and each one of those nieces and nephews will collect one-third (as there are three of them) of that two-thirds.

Per capita. Then we have "per capita," or "by head," which doesn't go down a generation but has the survivor of the immediate (same) generation collect. If you had in the same scenario—one surviving brother plus two nieces and one nephew—only the surviving brother would collect, and thus he would collect 100 percent.

Nine out of ten clients who come into my office prefer the traditional per stirpes distribution method. That goes away, however, if you pass intestate because New York's default rule is by representation.

I would never expect you to know this process or these rules. I always go through the rules of intestate with you (and go up and down the family tree in more detail than I have here). My clients are often surprised to see who has a real potential of collecting. If you want to dictate who gets your stuff and who doesn't get your stuff, you need to draft the proper documents.

The Siblings

I had a client with no children; she has three brothers and one sister. Once she understood what could happen if she didn't complete the planning process in a court-accepted manner, she got busy writing it up with me. Why? Because of her family dynamics and relationships.

She was close to her sister, and they lived together in a house she owned. She did not get along with her brothers. If she were to pass, she wanted to give the house to her sister because she didn't want her sister to be evicted. But if she passed without an estate plan, her sister would get 25 percent of the house, and her three brothers would each get 25 percent of the house. Her brothers, who had no involvement with her and were not nice to her, would get 75 percent. And if they wanted to bring a proceeding to force the surviving sister to sell her house, they could do so.

The only way to make sure your possessions go to the ones you intend is through an estate plan. Whether you do it as a trust or in a will, you must do something to protect those particular interests.

The Kids

The same thing is true when you have children. One of the biggest questions if you don't have an estate plan is "What happens to the kids?" No estate plan—dying intestate—means potential fights among family, all with good intentions and wanting the best for the child, but saying, "I'm better than you, so I'll handle this." Now you have created bad blood among good-intentioned people, and the court ultimately decides from the facts presented.

The only way to make sure your children are cared for by the one or ones you intend is through an estate plan.

That Matter of Tax

I had a client who was worth $14 million. I informed him that if he were to pass without an estate plan, his heirs would have to pay millions of dollars in estate tax to New York and big taxes to the feds. It was the words "millions" and "taxes" that got him moving.

We were able to put together an estate plan (unlike James Gandolfini's plan, whose story I will tell soon), with zero estate tax liability for his heirs. This was all because he sat with me to do some relatively simple planning.

And that is key: First-time clients and anyone without knowledge of what estate planning is believe it will be complex, convoluted, long to draw up, and so on. As the song goes, "It ain't necessarily so."

During your working years, you tend to think only of alleviating your personal tax burden for the current year.

Estate planning does that, too, while also reducing or eliminating the tax burden for your lifetime, not to mention the tax burden for your heirs.

The question I ask you and that I attempt to answer is, "What would the tax burden look like for your heirs?" We get some idea of that answer by adding up all your assets. If it's over the lifetime tax exemption thresholds (which I will talk about later), then you have a tax consequence (meaning that tax is going to be due). If it's under the thresholds, there is no tax consequence (no tax will be due).

Wouldn't you like to be in that "no tax consequence" category? I can tell you right now that your heirs would prefer that.

Who Manages What?

It's important to have a plan where you pick the right people for the job of representing your best interests when you're disabled or after your death (unlike Stan Lee, whose story is cautionary—I will tell his story soon too).

During estate planning, you're the one who decides and makes the choice of this "agent" and sets the criteria for that choice. It's about answering some basic questions:

- Who would be a great guardian for your minor kids?
- Who is savvy and trustworthy with money as a power of attorney (financial power of attorney) for your financial affairs?

- Who do you know who has a calm head on their shoulders and could serve as your medical or health care power of attorney (medical power of attorney)?

When you plan, you can choose those who will represent you. Remember that dying intestate means the court could pick anybody for those roles. It could be someone who looks good on paper, but in reality isn't the best choice for any number of reasons from religious faith to inability to manage complex affairs to bad blood between you during your lifetime.

I like to say that a plan is a formulated scheme to accomplish an end. Before we get to the "scheming" part, let's look once more at the consequences of "not scheming."

CHAPTER 4

And If You're Still Procrastinating . . .

It wasn't raining when Noah built the ark.
—Archbishop Richard Cushing

If you're still objecting to discussing and drafting an estate plan right now, let me give you some scary examples of what happens when a person with substantial assets passes intestate—or even when the person passes with estate plan documents that have been improperly drafted.

Those Special Cases

Here are three examples of what I mean, and who among your loved ones you should pay particular attention to in your planning:

Special needs. If you have a child with special needs, you must formally provide for the child. Plan now. Draft your estate plan to set aside what this child will need and want to have. Don't believe for a minute that a lump sum inheritance (without prior preparation) is the right way to plan for that child. It could knock your special needs child off vital government assistance forever (more on this in a later chapter).

Addiction. Perhaps you have someone who is unfortunately wrapped up in a substance addiction. You need to set forth your wishes in your will not only to provide for but to protect this individual, if that is your desire. You don't want that family member or beneficiary to suddenly have loads of money to spend on the addiction. You could hurt the family member who is an addict because now they have money to spend on their drug of choice (more on this in a later chapter).

Minor children. Parenting also means to plan for the unexpected, that is, for your death while you still have minor children. You don't want your minor children to inherit money without some guidelines. You also want to be able to choose who will raise and care for your children if you pass before they are of age and financially independent (more on this, too, in a coming chapter).

To the point of this last statement, I have twins who are currently thirteen years old. If, God forbid, my wife and I pass away, and they get my estate, they will get all of it as soon as they turn eighteen. Minor children can't inherit. You need to plan for the interim years and for when they come of age.

But will your children be "ready" to inherit at age eighteen? I remember when I was eighteen. What would I have done back then with a million dollars? Oh, boy, what a party year that would have been! I was never that wild child by nature, but still, what would a windfall of cash have done to my head? (More on your options for managing this later.)

Anyone can experience random or unforeseen circumstances. The press is full of stories about the early accidental death of a parent to minor children or dependent adult children. Parents with minor or special needs children need to consider right now what happens to the care of the children in the case of their own early death or incapacity.

Let me remind you that the default rules of intestate don't consider the mental or physical health needs nor the current and future financial situation of your heirs—minor children or others. Inheriting could blow up their needed government assistance eligibility or put an addicted heir's life in danger.

This is where discussions, information, and education with a trained estate attorney mastering the tax ramifications are invaluable as you decide how to organize your estate. An estate attorney will ask you the right questions and get you thinking about the various scenarios that might occur or need your special attention.

Estate planning is, in this case, about more than your financial assets, as you can see from my comments along the way. I've been describing one piece of the "when you're still living" planning that is part of an estate plan.

If you don't have an estate plan, you default. By default, I mean you let the courts apply the laws of intestate and decide who takes care of your children. There are two components of that:

1. Who has custody of the children? This is called the "guardian of the person."

2. Who manages the money for them? This is called the "guardian of the property."

I advise those of you with minor children to pick people for these two roles who would raise your children and manage the money in the manner that you choose. If you don't have an estate plan that lists guardians, it could lead to fights among the family members. The husband's side of the family and the wife's side are all trying to do the right thing to care for your child, and now each party will have to argue to the court why they are better than the others for this role.

A well-considered estate plan avoids interfamily conflict.

If the court has to choose the guardian because you didn't, the New York Surrogate Court will have its say about what goes on, to the point of creating long and drawn-out proceedings.

Ultimately, whether you name someone in an estate plan or not, the court will always operate in the best interest of your child. This is true. But in the process, having the court involved could put handcuffs on the guardian. Many expenses for the minor child would have to go through the court, and the guardian would have to justify any particular action before the court. You might not be able to move as quickly as you need to, whether for education or living costs. You may have to get prior approval. If the court is involved with choosing the guardian, every year there needs to be an accounting of expenditures for the child submitted to the court. It is time-consuming and costly.

If you pick your guardians and name them in a legal document, those encumbrances are reduced. The court may not require an annual accounting. If you pick someone and that person is shown to be or becomes a felon, the court could declare that person as inappropriate. The court will nonetheless give high deference to those you name personally.

Another reason to have an estate plan is that you pick who your executor or manager is. Some people are better at this than others—your sister Susan can't balance her checkbook, but your brother Jackson is an accountant. You will always know things like this better than the government.

Another consideration is the court can require your administrator or the manager of your estate to post a bond. That means they have to come out of pocket as an assurance that the administrator doesn't go to Las Vegas and put everything on black. But if you name an executor in your estate plan, the likelihood of the court requiring the bond is low.

An attorney will help you think through such circumstances for your estate plan, but you plan for it as opposed to closing your eyes, crossing your fingers, shouting a Hail Mary, and hoping the universe will do the right thing.

You have health insurance, insurance on your car, insurance on your house or rental apartment. Why? For the unforeseen—and to preserve your assets and wealth while the insurance carrier pays the damage, the bills, and the repairs. Look at your estate plan as another version of insurance. Don't delay any longer to consulting an estate attorney and drafting such plans.

James Gandolfini's Estate

Remember the popular TV show *The Sopranos*? James Gandolfini played Tony Soprano and won numerous industry awards in the process. He also acted in other films such as *Crimson Tide*, *All the King's Men*, and *Enough Said*, along with several roles in Broadway plays like *A Streetcar Named Desire*.

He passed away young, at age fifty-one. This New Jersey–born star was so beloved that Governor Chris Christie ordered flags flown at half-mast when he passed.

At his death in 2013, James's net worth was estimated at $70 million. He passed with a simple last will that left 80 percent of his estate to his sisters and daughter, and 20 percent to his wife. The 80 percent left to his sisters and daughter was subject to a combined federal and state tax rate of 55 percent, which resulted in the estate paying $30 million in death taxes.[5]

Thirty million dollars in estate taxes! Most people never see that kind of money in a lifetime. Uncle Sam essentially saw it all on the same day when Gandolfini passed.

Despite all his wealth and presumed access to the best attorneys, Gandolfini had an estate plan that consisted of a seventeen-page "simple will" (no trusts or other protective instruments) that made 80 percent of his hard-earned money subject to estate taxation.

The untimely (and poorly planned) death of celebrity James Gandolfini highlights the importance of strategic planning right now. In the realm of estate planning, let Mr. Gandolfini serve as a cautionary tale. No one wants to pay more in taxes than necessary. Much if not all of that $30 million should never have gone to Uncle Sam but to Gandolfini's loved ones.

---

5   "Mistakes of the Rich and Famous: James Gandolfini," Attypip.com, April 1, 2020, accessed November 11, 2024, https://www.attypip.com/mistakes-of-the-rich-and-famous-james-gandolfini.

And by the way, James Gandolfini signed his last will seven months before his death. He had been wealthy for a long, long time before that. Don't procrastinate. Plan. Plan early.

Stan Lee's Estate

Stan Lee was an American comic book writer, actor, and entrepreneur. Stan worked for the family business *Timely Comics* that famously morphed into *Marvel Comics*, and as most comic lovers and moviegoers know, *Marvel* turned into a film franchise whose superhero stories have captured the imaginations of young and old.

Stan had a net worth of $50 million at the time of his death in November 2018. He was ninety-five when he passed away in California. Stan's wife of seventy years passed away in July 2017, and at that time, Stan named his publicist as his agent under a power of attorney (POA).

It was alleged in the probate case that this publicist performed several unscrupulous acts:

- He dismissed Stan's lawyer and hired his own without disclosing the conflict of interest.
- He fired Stan's banker and transferred roughly $4.6 million out of Stan's account.
- He duped Stan into lending him $300,000.
- He bought an expensive condo for himself using Stan's money.

That isn't the whole list of acts the publicist allegedly committed during Stan's life and behind his back. The suit listed several causes of action, including financial abuse of an elder, fraud, and misappropriation of name and likeness. The publicist denied the allegations.

As I write this, a settlement has been reached in the case for an undisclosed amount, and now the probate case can proceed. There are, however, still some pending claims in the case against Stan's former attorney. Also notable is a criminal case Los Angeles prosecutors are pursuing against Stan's former business manager. That case has been pending since 2019, and he is facing several felony charges including theft, embezzlement, and false imprisonment of a senior.

Stan Lee's case highlights how important it is to be aware of and take steps to prevent, first, misappropriation of your wealth and assets and, second, senior abuse by individuals who were presumed to be acting in your best interests.

Stan was extremely wealthy, with access to virtually any resource or planning strategy, but still, he could and apparently did fall victim to fraud and abuse.

If you think that can't happen to you, think again. The Centers for Disease Control and Prevention states that out of those aged sixty and older, one in ten will experience elder abuse.[6] Elder abuse can take various forms, including physical abuse, emotional abuse, sexual abuse, financial exploitation, and neglect.

---

6   Hodes Milman, "Elder Maltreatment Statistics," Verdict Victory, June 6, 2024, accessed November 5, 2024, https://verdictvictory.com/blog/elder-abuse-statistics/.

I am passionate about addressing and preventing elder abuse. It's an issue that has become increasingly important for public health and safety. Having a professional and ethical elder law attorney handling your concerns can uncover and minimize the potential for abuse and fraud.

Don't procrastinate. Never hesitate to consult a professional estate attorney with tax expertise, and remember that you can get second and third opinions until you're comfortable with the professionals. Get referrals and references. You can "interview" your expert advisors before working with them on your estate plan—and you should.

If James and Stan had widened their search and interviewed a number of individuals, such as tax specialists, senior health care professionals, and elder law and estate attorneys, their stories might have ended much more advantageously, not just for the heirs as in James's case, but for themselves, as in Stan's case.

How do you want your story to end? Plan with me now to write that script yourself.

- The best time to put a comprehensive plan in place was yesterday.
- The second-best time is now.

PART 2

Tried-and-True, Tax-Savvy Inheritance Tax Strategies

Inheritance taxes are so high that the happiest mourner at a rich man's funeral is usually Uncle Sam.
—Richard Miller

My hope with the first chapters of this book was that I would scare you (yes, I admit it) into taking action as I showed you the dire and expensive consequences of not planning. Next, my goal is to demystify estate tax planning and show you how proper planning can quite neatly disinherit Uncle Sam.

Whether you're married or single, divorced or widowed, old or young, a parent or childless, what is fair is that you only pay your share of taxes and not a penny more. Proper and timely use of trusts, the will, and other strategies that are allowed by our tax code should and must be taken advantage of to protect your legacy.

Through thoughtful and properly documented estate planning, you're reducing Uncle Sam's share while increasing the share your beneficiaries can enjoy. You're also protecting your rights, your wealth, and your access to health care during your lifetime.

Remember the all-too-real stories of James Gandolfini and Stan Lee. Learn the lessons of their missteps. Without your planning, Uncle Sam feels totally comfortable serving himself up a huge percentage of your assets upon your death. Without this planning with trained, experienced professionals guiding you, you're leaving yourself and your spouse open to elder abuse, and you're leaving your assets open to theft, misappropriation, and loss.

In the chapters of part 2, I will discuss some real and practical strategies you can employ to avoid the missteps of Gandolfini and Lee. Using the strategies that apply to your particular and unique situation, you can protect yourself, protect your access to health care, and protect your inheritance to go to those individuals, organizations, and causes that matter to you.

CHAPTER 5

Essential Estate Planning Documents

*The government passes tax rules to fix problems
you didn't know you had in a way they don't
want you to understand.*
—Unknown

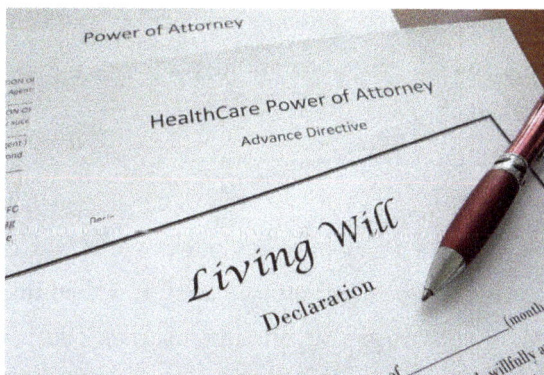

States and the federal government are particularly picky about using correct terminologies and formats in all estate documents. Attorneys are trained to be picky as well, so you're best off with an attorney like me whose area of practice is estate planning and taxation to draft all your documents.

Let's start with the documents that you will initially need as part of your estate plan's professionally drafted, legally binding documents.

The Power of Attorney

The power of attorney, or POA, is the document that allows you to pick the individual who will make your financial decisions. A durable POA allows the person you name to manage your finances on your behalf. Some of the most common powers allow this person to:

- Write checks
- Talk to the IRS
- Apply for government assistance on your behalf
- Get a handicapped parking plaque
- Make trusts
- Sell property

Note that a POA only has power while you're alive. That power expires when you pass away. It is then that your executor or your trustee or your administrator takes over.

A Health Care Proxy

Your health care proxy is a document in which you pick an individual to specifically handle your health and medical decisions in the event that you can't make those decisions yourself. This is the health care equivalent of the previous POA.

A Living Will

The document we like to do along with the health care proxy is called a "living will." Not the same as your last will, a living will serves to clarify your wishes and guide the decisions to be made by your proxy in the event you're in a vegetative state with no hope of recovery and being kept alive by machines. A living will avoids family members fighting about what happens, how, and when. Like dying intestate, with no living will, the case has to go to court, and the judge decides what it was that you wanted as opposed to you having a clear and documented statement as to your wishes.

If you're in a circumstance where machines are keeping you alive, and without them your passing is imminent, you can direct to have the machines turned off, have a do-not-resuscitate order, or go in the opposite direction (as one of my clients did) and direct that all extraordinary means to be kept alive are employed.

For Those Who Are Married

Here are the basic steps married people will be taking:

1. Get a clear idea of what your assets are since rules with regard to real estate, individual retirement accounts (IRAs), cash, and stocks can be different

for each category of asset. Do that first on your own, then fine-tune the list according to questions the attorney asks to unearth every last asset.

2. Take steps to reduce the tax impact or eliminate estate taxes and make sure your assets go where you want, as we discuss here in this book.

3. Along the way, be sure to properly name your beneficiaries. This applies to trusts, wills, insurance policies, bank and trading accounts, and your business.

4. Discuss with your attorney which professionally drafted legal documents you might need.

Let's dive a little deeper into each of those last three steps.

Taxes and Your Lifetime Exclusion Amount

Reducing the tax impact or eliminating estate taxes should be your goal.

Every American needs to account for the "federal basic exclusion amount," or the amount per taxpayer that can pass free of federal estate, gift, and generation-skipping taxes.

These amounts change periodically, and there is some uncertainty about this amount for 2026 as I publish this in early 2025. If Congress doesn't do anything before 2026, the federal exclusion amount drops from $13.61 million to $6.9 million. Yes, a significant drop. Yes, it will put more Americans over the exclusion amount as much less of your wealth is excluded. And yes, you can plan how to mitigate your federal tax bill.

"

The only difference between death and taxes is that death doesn't get worse every time Congress meets.

—Will Rogers

Federal Estate Tax Exclusion Is Based on the Year of Death

$11,580,000 in 2020
$11,700,000 in 2021
$12,060,000 in 2022
$12,920,000 in 2023

$13,610,000 in 2024/2025

Drops to approximately $7,000,000 in 2026

You have to be prepared to plan tax-wisely, not just as regards federal taxes but for your state taxes as well. Right now the federal piece states that if your assets go over the exclusion amount, you only get taxed on the overage. That means with a $6.9 million exclusion amount and assets worth $8 million, you will only get taxed on the $1.1 million overage.

New York has a special rule. In New York, if you're 105 percent over the exemption, you don't get taxed on just the overage, you get taxed from dollar one. That is an important distinction. If you're $347,000 over the $6.9 million limit, you're not going to be taxed just on that additional $347,000. You're going to be taxed on $6.9 million at a 16 percent state tax rate—or owe $1,104,000 in taxes to the great state of New York.

It's a huge amount, and you need to take it seriously. Getting beneath the threshold amounts, especially in New York, is important. With proper planning, you can.

Like the federal government, the states can change the exclusionary amounts when they need an influx of money or when a new official has been elected. Planning by someone with a solid tax background to deal with these situations is essential to preserving your wealth.

Your Beneficiary Designations

Another aspect of your estate planning is making sure you name beneficiaries on bank and trading accounts, life insurance policies, IRAs, annuities, trusts, and the like. But you must also periodically review your beneficiaries because, as we have observed, sh*t happens, and change is our only constant. A review should be triggered every time there is a "life change": a named beneficiary has passed away, you divorce, you remarry, a minor child reaches adulthood, you have a falling-out with a beneficiary or lose touch with them.

Clients tend to roll their eyes at this until I give real examples of how prior clients blew it—and often embarrassingly. A real example I have, alas, experienced more than once: You don't want your multimillion-dollar trading account assets to go to an ex-spouse you divorced twenty years ago when you've been with your current spouse for the past fifteen years. I've seen this happen to multiple clients. Ouch!

Stop reading and double-check your beneficiary designations right now. What better time?

When clients start to work with me—even when they thought they made the change—we'll put eyes on their designations and double-check them all. They will often discover errors in paperwork and changes they thought they had made but didn't.

I've seen trust situations where the insurance policy was made and beneficiaries named years earlier during a first marriage. The amount of paperwork around one of my client's divorce and remarriage had him believing he had, upon his second marriage, changed the beneficiary to the new spouse. Unfortunately, he wrote something wrong on the change forms. The insurance company caught it and sent him a letter requesting that he correct the problem. My client threw away the letter, thinking it was junk mail trying to sell him something. His beneficiary designation remained unchanged, still to the first spouse. Oops. Try to explain to wife No. 2 that the ex-wife is getting the multimillion-dollar policy.

I had a client who had gotten a policy before his marriage and had put his brother as beneficiary. He was married when he had his consultation with me. I made him confirm who was listed as beneficiary. We saw it was the brother and not his spouse. I had him rush to change the designation to his wife. When he understood that his brother would inherit and not the wife, he was in a panic—and grateful that I had caught this for him.

You should be looking at your trust documents and every beneficiary designation every three to five years to make sure it is up to date with your wishes and life circumstances.

Remember that the first job of estate planning is to make sure that your assets and possessions are going where you choose. The second job of estate planning is to plan to mitigate or eliminate the tax burden.

As the last piece of this puzzle, your attorney will draft the legal documents that allow you to achieve both those purposes. What those documents include will depend on your decisions, goals, and needs, because, contrary to popular opinion, there are no cookie-cutter plans.

CHAPTER 6

Credit Shelter Trust

Have a well-thought financial plan that is not
dependent upon correctly guessing what will
happen in the future.
—Barry Ritholtz

Some states say you have to have documentation from the court that certifies you are legally married, while other states say if you're together with someone under certain conditions, you're married by the common law.

In New York, there is no common-law marriage. Even if a couple has lived together for twenty years, they are not considered married in New York.

> If in doubt about your status, ask an attorney to verify it for you. It makes a big difference if you're married or not when it comes to inheritance planning.

Let me start with a bang here: When you pass away, you may leave an unlimited amount of assets to your surviving spouse, free of estate taxes. This is called the "unlimited marital deduction."

Yes, that seems unbelievable given how thirsty Uncle Sam can be.

As an extreme example of this rule, if Jeff Bezos wants to leave 100 percent of his billions of dollars to his wife, there is no estate tax consequence to her in the federal system. She would get it all, federal estate tax-free. States have different rules, but right now, Bezos could do it 100 percent with no federal estate tax consequence.

Things change, however, when the surviving spouse passes away with an estate worth more than the exclusion amount. Aha! Uncle Sam giveth with one hand but always taketh away with the other. The surviving spouse's estate will have to pay the inheritance tax on the exclusion overage amount. In New York State, depending on the amount, the estate could be liable for tax at dollar one and not just on the overage.

Credit Shelter Trust

This brings us to the first use of an irrevocable trust that I want to explore with you: Credit Shelter Trust[7] (CST) planning. A CST is a testamentary trust, in that it is created and funded after you pass away and through your estate plan (last will or within another trust).

With a CST, we're not concerned with the death of the first spouse, because of the "unlimited marital deduction." Let's kill off the husband first to see how this looks. When the husband dies, we establish the CST and put assets (cash, real property, etc.) into the CST. We limit the amount of assets to under the amount that can pass inheritance tax-free. The balance of the estate assets can be passed to the wife outright or in another trust. There is still $0 inheritance tax owed.

Now here comes the magic. The benefit of this plan materializes upon the death of the wife. The CST passes the assets to the beneficiaries under the estate taxable amount,

---

7   This trust is also called a family trust, AB trust, bypass trust, disclaimer trust, etc.

and the wife also passes her assets, which are under the estate taxable amount. Boom! We just eliminated the inheritance tax for the surviving spouse's heirs.

Let's look at some real numbers demonstrating the advantages of the CST.

First, let's see what happens without the CST.

Say we have a happy couple with a $10 million estate. The husband passes away in 2026 when we are at a $7 million threshold for the federal lifetime exclusion, with the typical "I love you will" that bequeaths everything to the wife. Then when the wife passes away, their children inherit. One hundred percent of assets pass to her, with no estate tax consequence to the surviving wife.

When the wife passes, that $10 million flows to her heirs (her children, in our example). In the federal scheme, using the projected 2026 exemption numbers, the first $7 million passes tax-free to the heirs, while the remaining $3 million is subject to the inheritance tax.

The 2026 estate tax rate is projected to be 45 percent, so upon the death of the second spouse, the estate will owe $1.35 million. The heirs would have to pay that amount in federal estate taxes.

That is the status with the federal exclusion rules. The heirs of the second spouse will be looking at a huge amount of tax to pay.

Can this be avoided? Yes. With the creation of the Credit Shelter Trust.

$7 Million Lifetime Exemption
Everything to Spouse Then to Children

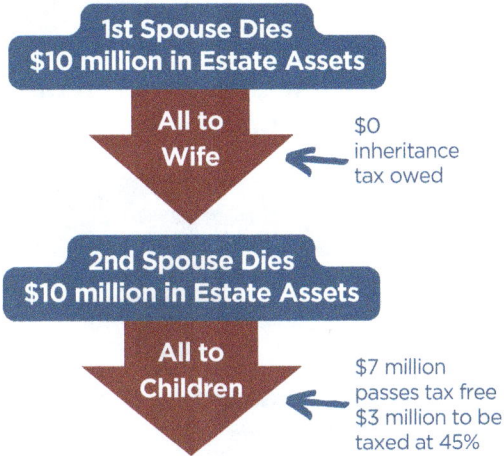

1st Spouse Dies
$10 million in Estate Assets

All to Wife

$0 inheritance tax owed

2nd Spouse Dies
$10 million in Estate Assets

All to Children

$7 million passes tax free
$3 million to be taxed at 45%

Estate Tax Owed: $1,350,000

Now let's say the husband planned and added a CST in his estate plan. When the first spouse passes away, the CST is created and $7 million is placed into the trust. The remaining $3 million goes to the surviving wife either outright or in another type of trust. Because the deceased spouse is putting $7 million in a trust, he's bequeathing less than the threshold amount. There is thus no estate tax consequence to fund the CST, and thanks to the unlimited marital deduction, no estate tax is due for the inheritance by the surviving spouse.

When the second spouse passes away, the CST passes $7 million to the children, and the wife passes $3 million to the children. They're both under the threshold limit. Boom! You just eliminated $1.35 million in taxes.

$7 Million Lifetime Exemption
Everything to Spouse Then to Children

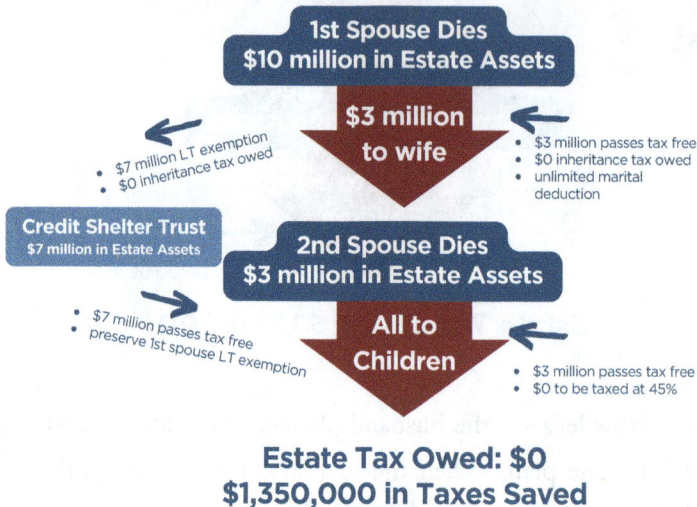

**1st Spouse Dies
$10 million in Estate Assets**

$3 million to wife

- $7 million LT exemption
- $0 inheritance tax owed

- $3 million passes tax free
- $0 inheritance tax owed
- unlimited marital deduction

Credit Shelter Trust
$7 million in Estate Assets

**2nd Spouse Dies
$3 million in Estate Assets**

- $7 million passes tax free
- preserve 1st spouse LT exemption

All to Children

- $3 million passes tax free
- $0 to be taxed at 45%

Estate Tax Owed: $0
$1,350,000 in Taxes Saved

When we do a CST, there are a couple of ways of approaching it as far as accessing the funds. First of all, the CST also establishes benefits to the surviving spouse, such as the ability to "invade" or access and spend the principal at will. Any invasion of principal becomes taxable income at ordinary income tax rates. The surviving spouse needs to declare that money as part of that year's income. Alternatively, we can give the surviving spouse what we call a "five-and-five" ($5,000 or 5 percent) so that they don't have to be asking a trustee for money. They can automatically get that amount.

The CST is also valuable for a young couple. There might be a fear that if the first one passes away when the children are still young, the survivor is going to take the money and run—go off with someone else and not take care of their kids. With a CST, you can mandate that the money goes to the biological children only so you can ensure that your children will get an inheritance.

Typically, we allow the surviving spouse to determine how much to put into the CST and how much they can take outright, based on the current year's exemptions and rules. Remember that I said the exclusionary amount might change in 2026. Uncle Sam writes the rules in pencil, so you have to be able to adjust to the current laws.

Also, the surviving spouse might think that if they put all $7 million into the trust, they won't have enough cash to live on. So instead of funding it at $7 million (or at the prevailing threshold limit), they can fund it with less and take more outright. The CST gives flexibility upon the death of the first spouse to determine how much to fund or not fund the CST.

In short, the CST preserves the first spouse's exclusion from estate tax—that $7 million exclusion in our example—for the death of the second spouse. Upon that second death, the $7 million exclusion applies to the heirs.

You don't want to be at a disadvantage because you haven't written the authority to create a CST into your estate plan. By putting the option into your plan, you can preserve that exclusion.

More Benefits of the Credit Shelter Trust

Are the benefits of the Credit Shelter Trust worth the trouble? The short answer is yes.

First, you avoid what might come to millions of dollars in estate tax—the $1.35 million in my above example. Additional benefits of a well-structured CST include shielding assets in the trust from creditors of the beneficiaries and offering a layer of security against potential claims. The CST preserves your wealth for future generations. In the event of a second marriage, the CST can flow through multiple generations.

The CST also gives control over distribution since you can specify terms under which the assets will be distributed as far as control and timing. If there is a distribution, it is ordinary income for the recipient. You work on the surviving spouse's situation to reduce or minimize their income taxes. The surviving spouse can receive income generated from the assets providing financial support without compromising the estate tax issues or without compromising the principal amount, which is intended for the next generation.

The CST also gives you flexibility in planning. The trust can be designed to accommodate changes in the law or in family circumstances and becomes a flexible tool in your plan. Beyond minimizing federal estate tax, the CST might reduce local or state estate taxes.

The assets held in the trust will pass without the need for a probate proceeding. With regard to those particular assets, the bequest passes quickly to the beneficiaries.

The CST can be structured to preserve the eligibility for certain types of income- and asset-based government assistance.

For those who are charitable-minded, the trust can be used to allocate a portion of the estate to charitable organizations, either during the lifetime of the surviving spouse or when the surviving spouse passes.

In short, the CST is a great way to preserve your exclusionary amount without having to worry about the strict deadlines and technicalities of portability, which may or may not be present in five, ten, or twenty years. This is not a living trust but a "testamentary trust" because it is created upon the death of the spouse. Be aware that providing for a CST doesn't mean you must create it. Don't miss the opportunity to provide for it in your estate plan.

Funding the Trust

How much to fund the CST is a matter of the amount of assets and also the federal exclusionary amount in the year you create the trust. Because those tax laws change so frequently, the surviving spouse seizes the currently prevailing exclusionary amount and decides from there how much to fund the trust.

Upon the death of the first spouse, the surviving spouse, the accountant, and the tax attorney will get together and determine the best amount to fund the trust—100 percent, 50 percent, or 0 percent. At that time, if there is only $2 million in the estate, you might decide it isn't worth it to have a CST, but that decision will be made at the death of the first spouse. Because you have provided for it, you have options.

The CST can hold (shelter) essentially every type of asset, except for IRAs. You can fund the trust to hold real estate, cash, stocks—whatever you want to hold. But your stop sign should be whatever the threshold amount is for tax exclusion.

CHAPTER 7

Irrevocable Life Insurance Trust

*If you don't have a Will or plan for your estate,
then the government has one for you.*
—Shez Christopher

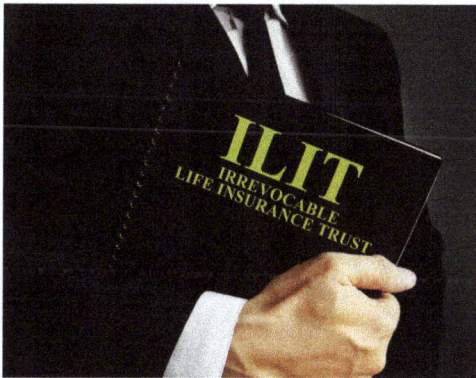

An irrevocable life insurance trust (ILIT) is an entity designed to be the owner and beneficiary of one or more life insurance policies. The trust is established to manage and distribute the proceeds of the insurance policies upon your death. By holding the insurance policy(ies), the real benefit is that it excludes that value from your taxable estate.

The catch is that you have to survive three years after the establishment of the trust for it to have that effect. Unlike a Credit Shelter Trust, you thus establish this ILIT before you pass away—and given the three-year constraint, the earlier the better.

What Is Your Taxable Estate?

The nature of Uncle Sam—any tax authority—is that when you make money, he's got to dip his beak and take a sip. To determine your taxable estate (and the size of Uncle Sam's sip), the IRS and your state government take a snapshot of all your assets. They don't care how they are titled, as long as you're an owner.

When we have a life insurance policy, the life insurance companies make a point to tell their clients that beneficiaries don't pay tax on the money they receive. What they don't tell you is that the death benefit becomes part of your taxable estate.

Now you know, and here's what that knowledge means: If your only asset is a $14 million life insurance policy, the taxing authority is going to chip away at the life insurance policy to get their estate taxes. If you die in 2026, you're over the $7 million exclusion exemption, and an inheritance tax will be imposed.

A template will off the internet doesn't do the work to calculate your taxable estate, but I do. If we see that your life insurance policy will cause you to have an inheritance tax consequence, I will advise you about creating an ILIT that will hold the policy and thus remove the insurance proceeds from your taxable estate. That is the magic of the ILIT.

Uncle Sam, on the one hand, allows you to exclude life insurance from the taxable estate. On the other hand, Uncle Sam tacked on a three-year survivorship requirement. Yes, it is excludable, but you have to survive for at least three years after creating and funding the ILIT to qualify.

As soon as I recognize that a life insurance policy has the possibility of pushing you over the limit, I will advise you to create an ILIT. Here's a real-world example. I had a client that had a $14 million estate that included $7 million in life insurance. If he were to pass away in 2026, there would be a $7 million exclusion limit. With $14 million in assets, he would be looking at an estate tax consequence of $3,150,000 (a projected 45 percent estate tax rate against the $7 million over the inheritance tax exclusion).

To stop that from happening, we created an ILIT that held his life insurance policies. After three years, his entire insurance policy death benefit will be excluded from his taxable estate. That means that if he passes away in 2026, I saved him $3,150,000 in inheritance tax.

$14 MILLION LIFE INSURANCE POLICY
In 2024, No Estate Tax Under $13.61 million

ILIT	**NO ILIT**
Less than three years old	$7 million over the Exclusion Amount
Still $7 million over the Exclusion Amount	
	Subject to Estate Tax at 45% or $3,150,000 tax paid by heirs
Subject to Estate Tax at 45% or $3,150,000 tax paid by heirs	

ILIT
Over three years old

No longer subject to Estate Tax

Benefits of the Irrevocable Life Insurance Trust

The main benefit of an ILIT is that you exclude the policy value from potential estate taxation. There are other benefits to such a trust:

- The ILIT gives you asset protection, so you're assured it goes through to your beneficiaries.

- The ILIT gives you control over distribution, meaning you can specify how and when your beneficiaries receive the death benefit, providing a structured financial future according to your wishes. Whether you spread out distribution over time or you want 100 percent distribution all at once is up to you.

- The distribution with an ILIT, as with all trusts, avoids probate and allows for a direct transfer of assets to your beneficiary. It could be held in a further trust for your beneficiaries or it could be distributed outright.

- The distribution and management of your proceeds through the trust is private; therefore, no one needs to know, other than the beneficiaries. Remember that a will, on its own, is a public record, but that's not the case with a trust.

- The ILIT allows you to easily accommodate changes in your beneficiary designations without having to go through whatever rules or technicalities the insurance company may have. You can change your beneficiary right through the trust and not necessarily through your insurance company.

- The ILIT provides professional management, which is important to grasp, as you're the one responsible for making and properly recording beneficiary changes. As with an insurance policy or bank account outside a trust, you need to properly change beneficiary designations.

- The ILIT allows flexibility and management with professional insight and ensures that the estate planning goals are met. The trustee may have the power to use cash from the insurance policy to purchase assets from your estate to provide your estate with liquidity.

CHAPTER 8

Annual Gift Tax Exclusion

A fool can earn money; but it takes a wise man to
save and dispose of it to his own advantage.
—Brigham Young

A major goal of estate tax planning is to reduce the amount of your wealth subject to taxation so you can keep more of it. I've already shown you that we achieve this with a Credit Shelter Trust and with irrevocable life insurance trusts.

The IRS and state taxing authorities do massive amounts of recordkeeping and research. Why? To make sure they get the maximum tax payment from you. Whatever the estate tax exclusion amount is when you pass away, the taxing authority will know how much of it you have used and how much remains and is taxable.

You need to do your own recordkeeping and organization of your finances (a.k.a. estate planning with all its tax-reducing or tax-eliminating strategies), to reduce your taxable estate.

That leads me to the next strategy called the "annual gift tax exclusion." It isn't a trust but a strategy; it is any gift you make to chip away at your lifetime exclusion. You can make gifts during your lifetime to reduce your estate and therefore your taxable wealth. You can make such gifts annually during your lifetime.

To take advantage of this strategy, you need to follow some simple rules. In 2024, the gift tax exclusion rules allowed you to gift $18,000 to as many individuals each year as you want without having to file a "gift tax return" and without you or the recipient having a tax consequence. Furthermore, if you're married, each of you can separately make $18,000 gifts, to potentially double the amount of your gift to $36,000 per person per year.

What happens, though, if you weren't aware of this rule and you gift your child $100,000? The IRS is record-keeping and notes that the first $18,000 of that gift passes with no need to declare it—and no reduction of your estate tax exclusion. The remaining $82,000 must be declared on a gift tax return. You're giving notice to the IRS and the state government that you've used up $82,000 of your estate exclusion.

We tax experts hate that. We don't want you to use any of your estate exclusion amount. We want you to retain as much of your lifetime exclusion as possible. In 2024, as I write this, the estate exclusion ceiling is $14 million. But we already know that it could be halved in 2026—all the way down to $7 million. You don't want to have already used up any of that lesser amount.

Annual Exclusion Gifting

Year of the Gift	EXCLUSION Single Donor	EXCLUSION Married Donors
2022	$16,000	$32,000
2023	$17,000	$34,000
2024	$18,000	$36,000
2025	$19,000[8]	$38,000

What About Gifts of Physical Assets?

The general rule is that the person who is giving the gift is the person who pays the tax and not the person receiving the gift. But what if you give something valued at or worth more than the 2024 $18,000 exclusion amount? Say that it has a value of $1 million, but it isn't cash. What then?

---

8   Estimated.

As an example, you're looking at gifting a $1 million house to your son. Your son doesn't get any income, he just gets the gift. Your son doesn't have to file on his income tax return that he got a gift valued at $1 million.

You, however, as the gift giver, are required to file a gift tax return stating that you gave $982,000 to your son. The first $18,000 passes according to the gift tax rules, and you declare the remainder, which is $982,000. The big computer at the IRS then records that you gave away $982,000, and notes that you filed a gift tax return. New York State and the IRS have computers that note these numbers next to your name. This year it said $7 million. Now they have changed it to only $6,018,000. You discounted your lifetime exclusion; it gets reduced.

It is even more than that with the New York tax authorities. This is because if you're over the estate threshold amount discussed in chapters 5 and 6, you have that fiscal cliff. You can go from owing just on what is over your life-time exclusion to owing 16 percent in New York State from *dollar one*.

That is why we tax advisors don't like you to have to file a gift tax return and use up any portion of the lifetime exclusion. We know that the ceiling could be lowered before your passing. We want you to preserve it all.

Gift Correctly

To use your annual exclusion to make gifts correctly to your children, you make gifts only in amounts within a limit set by the tax law in any given year to an individual. That way, you're (1) not incurring gift tax and (2) not using your donor's lifetime gift tax exemption.

Say you have a child who is married and has two kids. How can you gift what you believe is more significant money to your child's family in 2024 and still avoid the gift tax return issue—as well as not reduce your estate exclusion? You can gift $18,000 to as many individuals as you wish, so you gift $18,000 to your child, $18,000 to his wife, $18,000 to grandchild one, and $18,000 to grandchild two. Furthermore, if you're married, you and your wife can both do this and double your gifting ability.

You have gifted the more significant amount of $72,000 to your child's family without triggering a gift tax return—and without reducing your estate exclusion. In other words, there is no tax consequence on either you or your children. Win-win for everyone.

Gifting according to the annual rules allows you to make a systematic transfer of wealth to others without triggering tax.

George Steinbrenner's Estate

I have another celebrity example for you. The late billionaire George Steinbrenner is an interesting case on many levels.

You may or may not know that he acquired the New York Yankees in 1973 for $10 million. At his death, the Yankees were worth $1.6 billion. Talk about an increase in asset value.

Steinbrenner passed away in July of 2010. That was an extremely interesting year in federal estate–tax terms. It was an extremely wealth-preserving year too. In 2010, there was effectively no federal estate tax. This is the only year since World War II that this has been the case. In 2010, there was a temporary repeal of the estate tax for just that year as part of the Bush tax cuts of 2001.

Steinbrenner's estate was estimated at somewhere between $1.1 billion and $1.5 billion at his death. In tax terms, however, in that year it didn't matter a bit what his assets were. They were not subject to any estate tax. Not in 2010 when he passed away. If he had passed away six months later in 2011, however, his heirs would have owed around $500 million in federal estate taxes, as the federal estate exclusionary amount was increased to $1 million per individual at a top marginal tax rate of 55 percent.

The federal tax would have been over half of George's worth had he passed away eight months earlier or six months later.[9,10]

Put that crystal ball away. No individual can ever predict when he or she will (like George) have a fatal heart attack. Nor can your heirs (in spite of media noise at the time about George's children's motivations). What you can do is pass on wealth according to tax-favorable rules throughout your life through strategic estate and tax planning.

Let's look now at another aspect of giving and gifting.

9   Michael A. Craft, "Federal Estate Tax: Uncertain Times," Quinn Johnston, accessed October 19, 2024, https://www.quinnjohnston.com/federal-estate-tax-uncertain-times/.

10   Laurie Ohall, "Steinbrenner Fourth Billionaire in 2010 to Escape Taxes, If Not Death," Ohall Law, August 10, 2010, accessed October 19, 2024, https://ohalllaw.com/steinbrenner-fourth-billionaire-in-2010-to-escape-taxes-if-not-death/.

CHAPTER 9

Charitable Gifting

*We make a living by what we get, but we make a
life by what we give.*
—attributed to Winston Churchill

It has been my experience that many, many Americans are bighearted, or what I call charitable-minded. Far too many, however, don't plan their gifting with tax effectiveness in mind—and that tax effectiveness applies not just to you, the giver, but to the recipient as well.

Being bighearted doesn't have to cost you big-time at tax time.

Charitable Remainder Trust

The charitable remainder trust (CRT) is an irrevocable trust that distributes a fixed percentage of assets to a noncharitable beneficiary, with the balance (the "remainder") going to charity at a specified time. A CRT is designed to reduce the taxable income of a donor by first dispersing income to the beneficiaries of the trust for a specified period and then donating the remainder of the trust to the designated charity.

This strategy reduces your taxable income by first showering beneficiaries with income for a set period, then passing the remaining assets to your chosen charity. It's like having your cake, eating it, giving a slice to your friends and family, and then donating the cake stand to charity.

One of the primary advantages of a CRT is its impact on inheritance tax. By transferring assets into a CRT, you remove them from your estate, potentially lowering your estate tax liability. This can result in significant tax savings, especially for estates that exceed the estate tax exemption limit.

How does that look? Let's say you have a commercial storefront property and you also own a fourplex residence. Both are income-producing assets. You can put both income-producing assets (and others) into this CRT. During your lifetime, you get the benefit of the income from the assets, while the charity doesn't get anything. Not yet.

As another example, say you're living off your Social Security benefits and your work pension. In addition, you have five income-producing houses where one house is pushing you over the exclusionary limit. You create a CRT. You put one $2 million house (or all of them) inside the CRT and still collect the income from it—you have it to spend any way you like. Your life isn't affected. It's when you pass away that the assets in the CRT go to charity.

A CRT is a way to reduce your taxable estate to below the estate tax threshold.

Keep in mind that if your only asset is one house and you put it into a CRT, your kids or other heirs aren't getting it upon your passing. The charity will be the recipient.

The CRT is a good vehicle for high-wealth people to remove some of their and their heirs' tax liability.

There are many benefits to using the CRT strategy. You get an instant income tax deduction when you transfer assets into a CRT, as it is immediately counted as a charitable donation. A CRT can sell appreciated assets without incurring capital gains tax, allowing the full value of the assets to work for both the beneficiaries and the charity. Your beneficiaries get a steady flow of income for a set term or for life, and assets in the CRT bypass probate. You can mix and match beneficiaries, term lengths, and income distribution types all according to what you're passionate about.

Discuss this strategy with me, however, because once your assets fund the CRT, they're out of your hands and destined for charity, not your heirs. Note that CRTs often require a substantial initial contribution to be effective and that setting up and managing a CRT is complex and comes with continuing costs and ongoing oversight to comply with IRS rules and regulations.

You should also look closely at your financial needs: Will the fixed income generated keep up with inflation? Will it be enough for you over time, combined with any other income you have? The trust's assets, depending on their nature, could face investment risks, which can threaten your income payments and the charitable remainder goals.

Those who will get the most benefit using a CRT:

- Individuals in a higher income tax bracket seeking tax relief

- Individuals who have a strong philanthropic desire to support charitable causes

- Individuals who own highly appreciated assets and are concerned about capital gains tax

- Individuals who desire an additional income stream for themselves or their heirs

- Individuals who wish to leave a legacy and make a significant impact on a charity or the community

Charitable Lead Trust

A charitable lead trust (CLT) is a different trust instrument to consider for the fulfillment of your charitable goals and your tax-efficient estate planning. This sophisticated trust isn't for everyone, however, given its pros and cons.

First, what is a CLT exactly? The CLT is an irrevocable trust designed to support charitable organizations through a predetermined income stream for a specific term. At the end of the term, the asset is transferred to your heirs. This is the opposite of the CRT where you get the income generated by the asset during your lifetime, and when you pass away, the charity receives the asset.

You thus need to fund the CLT with an asset that is generating income. You also need to set a term during which the charity will receive this income, and terms can be long—for instance, twenty years. At the term set out in advance, both the asset and the income come back to the heir (not to the charitable organization).

Your financial needs are, again, a main consideration when considering this type of trust: You no longer receive the benefit of the income of the assets that you're putting in during the term, whether it's rent from a house or a building, stock dividends, or interest in a bank. Whatever income that asset generates is out of your estate now and, for the term, goes to the designated charity.

How could this look for you? Let's say you want to support charities that rescue animals. You've been donating $30,000 a year for many years to these various pet rescues. But you now think about that piece of real estate generating almost that exact amount of income—you understand that if you created a CLT and funded it with that piece of real estate, your giving goal would be fulfilled each year through the trust. You know that you don't need that income to support the real estate or to live your life. You formalize the donation through a CLT.

Those who are optimal candidates for a CLT:

- Individuals who have a history of significant charitable giving

- Individuals who possess substantial assets

- Individuals who want to minimize estate and gift tax impacts

- Individuals who don't need the income generated from the asset funding the CLT

- Individuals who want the asset to revert to the family when they pass

A CLT will provide a structured way to contribute significantly to charitable causes over time. It allows you to witness and enjoy the benefits of your philanthropy during your lifetime. The trust's term, beneficiaries, and asset types can be tailored, offering flexibility to align with your personal and philanthropic goals.

Putting the asset in the CLT removes it from your estate and thus minimizes inheritance tax since the CLT assets are considered transferred out of your estate into the trust. Assets placed in a CLT are also shielded from creditors, providing another type of protection.

Assets growing at a rate surpassing the IRS's assumed rate can result in a larger inheritance, tax-free. If drafted correctly, when you pass, that appreciation is wiped away. We will speak later about "basis step-up," but simply stated, the fair market value of the assets readjusts to the date of death and the capital gains is erased should your heirs sell the asset. You have to draft the CLT properly to ensure this outcome.

Understand that this is an irrevocable trust. Like any irrevocable trust, there is no turning back. It is Moses and the Ten Commandments chiseled into a stone tablet. When that property goes into the trust, you're giving up the income stream; it's essentially gone for good. That's why you have to be aware of what your cash flow needs are now and project them into the future.

The reduction in your estate reduces the potential estate tax. During the term, you claim a reduction of your income tax because you're donating the income to charity. A high-net-worth family will want to make sure of the income and tax impact on the children when choosing and setting up this trust.

We will need to discuss your goals in depth so we can determine together whether this is the right vehicle for your giving. The commitment to charity is fixed and must continue irrespective of personal circumstances. Remember that a CLT implies continuing costs because of the complexity of establishing and administering it, and it requires ongoing tax reporting and code compliance updates as needed. A professional trustee is strongly recommended to avoid mismanagement of the assets in the CLT.

Donor-Advised Funds

A donor-advised fund (DAF) is a charitable investment account established at a public charity. Thus, this option is not another trust, but an account—a philanthropic fund administered by a public charity. The DAF administrators are often called "sponsoring organizations" and can be community foundations, national charitable organizations, or the charitable arms of financial institutions.

Individuals and families can create a DAF, just like organizations and businesses. A family DAF can be used to involve family members in philanthropic decisions. The ideal candidate for a DAF is someone who seeks to make significant charitable contributions while also enjoying the flexibility of distributing those funds over time.

"Donor advised" means you can recommend where that money goes over the course of time. That is, you can contribute cash stocks or other assets and then make suggestions on how you like those assets to be distributed to charities of your choice. You need to be comfortable with being one step removed from the decision—you're an "advisor," not the final decision-maker. It is, in the end, the governing body of the DAF that decides on the recipients of the donations.

This should lead you to pick the fund carefully since it is the board that determines which tax-exempt charity receives donations—not you. In a DAF, you can't direct the money to go specifically to St. Jude, the animal shelter on Third Street, or to Catholic Charities. It's the board that says, "These are our purposes; this is where the money goes." So it's not a direct contribution.

In other words, if you want to donate to a specific charity, a DAF wouldn't be the vehicle to choose. If you have really big assets, let's say, and you want to be more directly involved in the choice of the recipients, the charitable remainder trust or the charitable lead trust might be better options for your giving.

The DAF allows you to make a charitable contribution and receive an immediate income tax deduction. Donor-advised funds accept various types of assets, including stocks, real estate, and more. When donors contribute to a DAF, they surrender ownership of the assets. This is a way that many smaller donors can participate and aggregate their contributions for greater impact.

The DAF can simplify your charitable giving, consolidate your donations, and potentially grow your contributions tax-free as a centralized platform for all your charitable donations. This is also a cost-effective way of organizing your giving: The administering charity handles all receipts and recordkeeping.

Assets in the DAF grow tax-free, potentially increasing the impact of your giving. Donor-advised funds allow you to make anonymous donations, if desired. Many DAFs offer various investment strategies to increase your contributions.

The DAF is particularly beneficial when you are in high-income years looking for immediate tax deductions. You may use the DAF to "play the tax brackets" from year to year. If you're in a high tax bracket, or in one year you get a huge bonus or a huge commission, and you're skyrocketing upward into higher tax brackets, you could do it as a way of reducing a sudden influx of taxable income.

In addition to the need to pick the DAF carefully, there are downsides to consider. Understanding and navigating DAF policies can be complex. Donor-advised funds charge annual fees based on the fund's size, and some DAFs require a minimum initial contribution. Grants can only be made to qualified 501(c)(3) tax-exempt public charities. Recommendations for grants can be delayed at the discretion of the administering charity. The increasing popularity of DAFs has also led to more scrutiny and calls for regulation.

Please keep in mind that there is no benefit of the asset to you or your heirs; it is only your tax benefit. Unlike tools like the charitable lead trust or the charitable remainder trust, the DAF does not provide a stream of income to you or your heirs. It is 100 percent philanthropic.

Private Foundations

Trusts and private foundations are both legal structures used for asset management and charitable giving, but they have some key differences.

The private foundation is its own separate legal entity, similar to a corporation but without shareholders. The private foundation is a true legacy device. It might be a good vehicle for those with substantial assets who are concerned about inheritance tax mitigation and leaving a charitable legacy.

You have likely heard of a number of private foundations. The Ford Foundation was established in 1936 and is one of the oldest major foundations in the country. It works on issues of social justice, human rights, and civic participation. The Bill & Melinda Gates Foundation was founded in 2000 to focus on global health, education, and poverty reduction.

If you think about those or the Carnegie Mellon Foundation or the Rockefeller Foundation, don't think you can't do this too. Even with $1 million, or with only a house that is paid off with no one you want to bequeath it to when you pass away, a private foundation is a great option. If you've been involved in charities or want to have a legacy, whether it's a scholarship or education or people in their alma mater or the protection of animals or whatever, this is enough to bequeath.

Your private foundation is your legacy, showcasing your values and philanthropic goals and continuing to make a lasting mark on the communities and causes you care about. The foundation will live on past you and do works in your name.

If you have a continual history of charitable gifting during your lifetime or have a particular charity you're closely intertwined with, I will talk with you about a private foundation. If you don't have any heirs, are a widow or widower, or are not close with your family, I will likewise start a conversation about private foundations.

In your estate documents, we would include a clause giving a percentage or all your assets to a tax-exempt private foundation to be established on your death in your name to carry out a certain charitable purpose. The trustee or executor then establishes it as a tax-exempt private foundation, and it continues to do good works or bestow charitable gifts on your behalf in perpetuity.

I like to call this your "get out of purgatory early" card. If you're on the borderline whether you're going to get to heaven or have to spend an extended amount of time in limbo, but you have a charitable foundation that is continuing to do good work on your behalf, maybe this will push you over the hump and get you into heaven quicker.

While you have read that not all trusts and vehicles may be funded with IRAs, this one can. You could fund the foundation with your IRAs. If you have a direct payment from your IRA into a charity or charity foundation, then that income is not on your regular income tax return as you're donating it to charity. During your lifetime, you can establish a foundation to take that unneeded IRA amount, and it will lower your income tax. As you might guess with Uncle Sam, there are specific rules and regulations that apply in this latter solution, but it reduces your current income tax, and it establishes this foundation for your charitable works. Then upon your death, it will reduce your inheritance tax.

Additionally, a private foundation is a legacy device that you could have family members run. Depending on its size, they could be paid to do so (again, there are the rules and regulations as to how to do that correctly).

Some of the downsides of a private foundation are around its management. Foundations are tax-exempt, so they're subject to strict IRS rules and regulations that require rigorous recordkeeping and reporting. As just one example of a rule, you must give away a minimum amount annually for charitable purposes. A private foundation can involve significant administrative and legal costs. Failure to comply with IRS regulations can result in tax penalties.

Nonetheless, if you're interested and have assets in mind that could fund it, let's discuss the option to create a private foundation.

Charitable Bequests or a Foundation?
There is a difference between continuous giving after you pass away and giving one time to a list of charities when you pass away.

If your estate documents state you will give 50 percent to cancer prevention research and 50 percent to soup kitchens, that's a one-and-done bequest. The charitable organizations receive that money in that one year and that's it.

If you have a private foundation, the donations happen perpetually. A foundation will continue to provide support annually to the causes you have designated. That isn't a one and done. That's a long-lasting legacy.

Establishing a foundation, a charitable corporation like a 501(c)(3), a DAF, or a trust are distinct forms of vehicles with different effects. A private foundation lasts in perpetuity. A DAF is a specific type of brokerage account that puts your money in with other money and gives it to the charity of your choice as a one-and-done transaction. A CRT is a one and done because once you pass away, the property is removed from the trust and goes to the charitable organization.

Your private foundation is your legacy. These other plans, while they are effective in reducing your taxable estate, are all essentially one-and-done bequests.

Part of the charitable giving and legacy discussion I've had with clients includes the question "How much is there to leave?" If it's a significant amount, maybe you want to do a private foundation and have something that lasts, rather than just a one and done. You will have a real legacy device. But if it's $50,000 or $100,000, it's best to do a one-and-done bequest.

A client of mine needed advice on giving, and her desire was to support a long-established 501(c)(3) music organization. She wanted to give a lump sum every year to the organization and make sure it continued to happen in an ongoing annual manner after she passed away. She asked, "Which of these vehicles does that?" It is hands down the private foundation. It is perpetual. I explained we could write that at least 20 percent of earnings on the foundation's assets were to be donated per year to that qualified organization as long as it existed as a qualified organization.

Another client of mine was passionate about taking care of rescued animals. He wanted to support one or more pet rescue charities every year in the amount of at least $10,000 a year. We set up the foundation so that at least that amount went to pet rescue organizations until either the organization(s) didn't exist anymore or the money ran out. He could name the pet rescue charity, and then if that animal rescue closed, the foundation would look for another similar animal rescue to support.

Note that the goal of giving by the foundation is not to have the money run out, but rather to do work on the inside of the foundation to keep it funded—either from fundraising, investing assets for income, or accepting donations from others.

All these charitable giving vehicles have a place. You need to discuss your goals and then, depending on the assets you have to support your charitable giving goals, we can choose the appropriate vehicle.

Comparing Charitable Giving Vehicles:
CRTs, CLTs, DAFs, and Private Foundations

	Goal	Benefits	Considerations
Charitable Remainder Trusts	Designed to convert assets into a lifetime income stream for the donor, with the remainder going to charity	Immediate income tax deduction Reduce size of taxable estate Income stream during trust term	Does not revert to heirs upon donor death Limited beneficiary flexibility Cannot be revoked
Charitable Lead Trusts	Designed to donate income to a charity for a specified term, after which the remaining assets revert to the donor's heirs	Immediate income tax deduction Reduce size of taxable estate Assets go to heirs upon donor's death	Does not revert to donor who outlives trust Loss of income stream Financial effect on beneficiaries
Donor-Advised Funds	Designed to allow donors to make charitable contributions, receive immediate tax deductions, and recommend grants over time	Immediate tax deduction and potential for tax-free growth Simplifies the process of managing charitable giving Provides options for anonymity in donations	Donors advise but ultimately do not control the final grant decisions Potential minimum contribution requirements
Private Foundations	Designed to allow donors to establish a legacy and minimize inheritance taxes after death	Legacy and family involvement allowing for the continuation of charitable giving across generations Mandates specific causes or organizations that align with the donor's passion Removes assets from inheritance taxation and can continue activities within a tax-exempt structure	Private foundations are subject to strict regulatory oversight Continuing costs related to compliance, management, and activities Limited anonymity because annual filings that include foundation's finances, grants, income, expenses, etc, are publicly available

CHAPTER 10

Shield, Heal, and Defend Against Long-Term Care Costs

The trouble is, you think you have time.
—attributed to Buddha

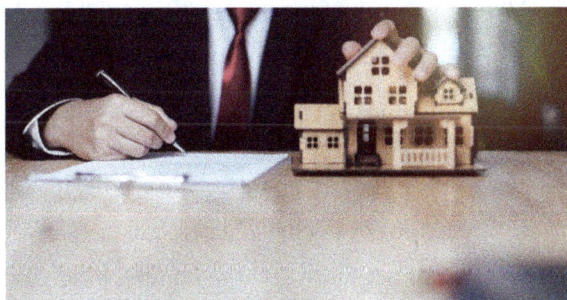

I have to go back to my earlier tactic here and scare you first before I calm your fears.

A sixty-five-year-old American retiring in 2024 can expect to spend an average of $165,000 on health care and medical expenses throughout retirement. This spending estimate has more than doubled since 2002 and increased by nearly 5 percent from 2023.[11]

This last statistic should make you not only ask, "How much more will the costs increase by the time I need help?" but also ask, "Will I need the *average* amount of spend to care for myself—or much, much more?"

For many Americans who don't have a high net worth, this expenditure can ruin their retirement simply because their retirement funds earmarked for daily expenses are decimated by medical costs.

There are several reasons why medical costs decimate American wealth, not just for anytime accidents that can occur to anyone, but especially in our elder years:

- Underestimating or not estimating total potential costs (the average spend might be less than your spend).

- Realizing you don't know how much health care is funded out of pocket (20 percent, in case you wondered) because you have no idea which care isn't covered by your insurance plan—and when you need it, it's from your pocket. The usual culprits are dental, vision, and drug costs.

---

11   "Fidelity Investments® Releases 2024 Retiree Health Care Cost Estimate as Americans Seek Clarity Around Medicare Selection," Fidelity, August 8, 2024, accessed November 7, 2024, https://newsroom.fidelity.com/pressreleases/fidelity-investments--releases-2024-retiree-health-care-cost-estimate-as-americans-seek-clarity-arou/s/7322cc17-0b90-46c4-ba49-38d6e91c3961.

- Having no clue what long-term health care entails, costs, or what services are under your insurance plan, which takes you back to the previous point of how much will need to be funded out of your pocket.

Medical debt among older adults is significant and not projected to decrease anytime soon in our country. As of 2020, 7 percent of Americans over sixty-five (nearly four million people) had unpaid medical bills totaling nearly $54 billion collectively. This represents a 20 percent increase from 2019 to 2020.[12]

What about you when your health care needs intensify? The health care industry is known for its annual price increases. The insurance industry follows suit. Inflation is another big hit.

Here's where I calm you down: There are solutions that protect your wealth and therefore your legacy as well as ensure you have the means to receive and pay for the health care you need and want.

The downside: You have to plan years in advance. Call me up—now.

Medicare Versus Medicaid

Before we get much further in this topic of long-term health care cost planning, I have to talk about the difference

---

12   Jon Marcus, "Over 65? Beware Medical Debt," AARP, September 22, 2023, accessed November 7, 2024, https://www.aarp.org/money/credit-loans-debt/info-2023/unpaid-medical-bills-for-older-adults-grow.html.

between Medicare and Medicaid. You need to understand the difference between the two—whether right now as you deal with a parent's health care management or later, for yourself.

People get the two programs confused all the time. Here, in relation to health care needs in retirement, is the basic difference:

- Medicare is general health insurance for those aged sixty-five and older who pay into the system.

- Medicaid is long-term health care insurance.

Another difference is that when you're sixty-five, you start paying a monthly Medicare health care insurance premium, generally deducted from your Social Security benefit. We don't pay premiums for Medicaid, as it is paid for differently when an individual needs it.

How Medicaid is paid for needs to get your attention.

How it is paid may affect your wealth and your ability to leave a legacy.

If my mom is over sixty-five and has Medicare for general health insurance, Medicare coverage will pay for the doctor visits, her prescription drugs, and going to the emergency room and the hospital in case she has some medical emergency.

Where you get confused is that Americans of any age who are unable to pay for health care can be on a Medicaid program that pays for those services but in a limited manner.

Here's the rub. My mom's Medicare coverage won't pay for long-term health care. Medicare doesn't cover such long-term needs such as home health care or nursing home care. Under most insurance policies, including Medicare, you can't stay in the hospital forever. They don't offer coverage for long-term care.

The hospital is for emergencies and the care you need in the immediate aftermath. If you have a heart attack or a stroke, you get into a car accident, or you break your arm, it's an emergency, and you go to the hospital and may stay a day, a week, or longer to stabilize your health in the aftermath of the incident.

Hospital care is only until the emergency is over. In the hospital, your health insurance (depending on the policy's terms) will cover your stay and what goes on in the hospital as far as the medical needs, medications, or surgeries, and then afterward for the follow-up in-office doctor visits, as well as whatever drugs they prescribe you. Your Medicare, or your health insurance, will pay for that.

When the emergency is over, either you're sent home or you enter a residential health rehabilitation center because you're still not well enough or able to go home. Your Medicare, or your health insurance, will pay for a limited amount of time for you to be in that rehabilitation center. Typically, it's about 180 days, depending on the policy. Insurance people call 180 days and less "short-term." After that, you may be entering into what insurance defines as "long-term" care needs.

That's where, starting on day 181, you will pay for your care out of your own pocket (known as "self-pay"), or you will have long-term care Medicaid in your health care picture (if you're eligible and have been accepted for coverage), or you have subscribed to a long-term care (LTC) insurance policy that kicks in. Like self-pay, LTC is a private and personal decision on your part. Without preplanning, however, most won't have that LTC insurance coverage.

If you don't have LTC insurance and you have assets that are over and above what Medicaid deems to be the poverty line, you have to pay for your long-term care yourself as your only remaining option.

That's the difference between Medicare and Medicaid.

I explain this difference to clients who tell me, "We don't need to plan for Medicaid. That's for the indigent. We have money. We're not poor." It's the long-term health care piece of your thinking and planning that people don't understand. It's the Medicaid piece of the puzzle that baffles them.

So You Want to Self-Pay for Long-Term Care?

I get it. When all is said and done, you shrug and say to yourself that you've got plenty of money, and if needed, you can self-pay—pay out of your pocket—for long-term health care when the need arises.

As a self-paying patient, you have choices. You can opt for better, more customized, personal care paying out of pocket because that is how and when you choose the facility you receive care from and the level of care you receive (and pay for).

This is different from Medicaid. Another little-known aspect to Medicaid to consider: You must only use Medicaid-approved personnel and facilities. When you're on Medicaid long-term care, the program decides the extent of your care. The decision is out of your hands and out of your loved one's hands. "Take what you get" is the Medicaid approach.

As in other aspects of planning I've already discussed, you want to be the decision-maker. You don't want Uncle Sam, the courts, or the Medicaid authorities to decide in your place.

There isn't anything wrong with Medicaid agencies or Medicaid personnel. I like to say that planning for health care is like dating. There are caregivers you're going to like and some you're not going to like, and if you're paying out of pocket, you can use whoever you want. If you're using Medicaid to pay, you must use Medicaid agencies, services, and personnel. More choices give more opportunities to find the perfect fit for you.

It's not that the Medicaid agencies don't have good people or that they're corrupt or anything of the sort. It's just that they offer you a limited pool. By privately paying, you're going to get better care. You get to pick any agency you want and any people you want, and you can also choose care for as long as you want and choose any facility you want.

Be aware that, statistically speaking, the average stay in a long-term care facility is three years per individual. If the cost to you at the time you're admitted is $150,000 a year to be in the facility of your and your family's choice, that's $450,000 for your average stay of three years. Again, you must ask, Will you need more than the average-length stay?

Note some costs that apply as I write this in 2024:

- Private room in a nursing home: This is typically the most expensive option, with costs on average up to $9,034 per month.

- Assisted living facility: The median monthly cost for a one-bedroom unit in an assisted living facility is on average $4,500.

- Home health aide: For those preferring to receive care at home, the median monthly cost for a home health aide is on average $5,148.

Remember that those are today's (2024) estimated costs, and they are only averages or medians of nationwide numbers. They certainly won't be what you pay in, say, fifteen or twenty years when you need the facility and the care it provides. Genworth has estimated that in just six short years, by 2030, a private nursing home room could cost $11,787 per month.[13] Again, that's an average in a nation that has pockets of extremely high costs of living and pockets of greater affordability.

Now, consider that you and your spouse both need long-term stays at the same time. That's a bottom-line financial need of $900,000 at today's estimated prices for you both for three years. You're going to eat up a good portion of your estate in those three years (and who's to say it won't be many more years than that). Even if your estate is $3 million, do you really want 30 percent of it to be eaten up on medical expenses alone?

The Rules and Your Plan

Medicaid is a federal long-term care insurance program that is administered by the states. The program follows some basic rules around eligibility and are about the limits to the income you may possess and the limits to the value of the assets you may possess.

In short, if you have too much income and assets, you need a plan to fall within the criteria for eligibility.

I'm a New York–admitted attorney, so remember that my discussion is going to be focused on New York rules. But whichever state you hang your hat, that's the state whose rules control the criteria. Although Medicaid is a federal program, it's run by the states.

---

13   Alison Tobin, "Long-Term Care Insurance Costs," Money, December 26, 2023, https://money.com/long-term-care-insurance-costs/.

Medicaid Planning Is Legacy Planning

Because of those eligibility rules, we want to protect your assets but also help you qualify (or become eligible) for Medicaid long-term care.

The reality about asset protection and Medicaid eligibility: The goal of Medicaid asset protection is not to give *you* any benefit; it's planned for the benefit of *your heirs*. In other words, Medicaid planning is legacy planning. I hear you now: "Stephen! We thought this was about long-term health care?" It's that too. And stop yelling at my book.

Bear with me while I explain.

I've encountered clients who are "house rich and cash poor." They have a million-dollar house and $100,000 or less in the bank. The other type of client is the adult who comes to me with the parents who have a house and substantial assets where those parents suddenly need significant amounts of long-term (for instance, nursing home) care.

Planning is important in both cases not only to get that health care you need but to protect your assets and your legacy too.

My philosophy when it comes to your elder health care is this: We have a dual focus on (1) asset protection and (2) health care insurance planning. The first item, protection, is your insurance of inheritance. The second, Medicaid, is a significant part of your health care insurance plan.

Think about it: Is there anything in your assets, your portfolio, your property that you own, whether it be real property or cash property, that you want to ensure goes to your children? This is your legacy, and you need to protect it for them. Without proper health care planning, that legacy might dwindle to nothing for your heirs.

Medicaid planning is legacy planning.

What can the discussion with me look like for you? Here are two scenarios.

First case: I had clients that owned a $2.5 million brownstone in Brooklyn where they lived on one floor and rented out the other two floors for income. They also had some IRA accounts and $600,000 in non-IRA nonqualified accounts (maybe a brokerage account or two). They were concerned about passing the brownstone and at least $100,000 to each of their three kids without having to worry about spending down these assets on long-term medical costs. In other words, they wanted to leave this legacy to their children.

Second case: I had clients who came in for tax planning, and we spoke about their long-term health care concerns. They had $3 million in the bank, all cash. No property or other assets of value. No children. No family they liked. They asked me, "Why would we need to go on Medicaid?" I responded that they didn't. I did recommend looking into a long-term care insurance policy. I suggested when the need occurred, to move into a long-term care facility in the Hamptons overlooking the ocean, or one across the country in Beverly Hills. "Spend it on yourselves," I said. "You can't take it with you, as they say." We also discussed creating a private foundation to create a legacy.

The "I'm Healthy!" Argument

The Department of Health and Human Services projects that more than 56 percent of those turning sixty-five will need some sort of long-term health care services.[14] Other estimates are even higher:

- The Health and Retirement Study results show that 70 percent of adults who survive to age sixty-five will develop severe long-term care needs before they pass away.[15]

- The Administration on Aging estimates that at least 70 percent of people who are sixty-five today will require care in some context.[16]

We don't have a crystal ball, but you could be among the seven out of ten readers of my book needing long-term care—and probably via Medicaid. You owe it to yourself to read a bit more about what to do about your planning.

Let's now see about Medicaid eligibility.

---

14   Eva Rothenberg, "More Than Half of Older Americans Will Need Long-Term Care. Many Can't Afford the Rising Cost," CNN, September 17, 2023, https://www.cnn.com/2023/09/16/business/aging-population-insurance-costs/index.html.

15   Richard W. Johnson, "What Is the Lifetime Risk of Needing and Receiving Long-Term Services and Supports," Office of the Assistant Secretary for Planning and Evaluation, April 3, 2019, https://aspe.hhs.gov/reports/what-lifetime-risk-needing-receiving-long-term-services-supports-0.

16   Claire Samuels, "Long-Term Care Statistics: A Portrait of Americans in Assisted Living, Nursing Homes, and Skilled Nursing Facilities," A Place for Mom, September 13, 2023, https://www.aplaceformom.com/senior-living-data/articles/long-term-care-statistics.

Eligibility

Eligibility for Medicaid long-term care benefits and services is based on two factors. First is a health eligibility of two types. Second is your financial eligibility.

Health Eligibility

To determine health eligibility, the first type of activities focuses more on the physical aspects, while the second type is around mental capacity.

The first type of health eligibility is the activities of daily living (ADLs). Can you perform the functions of daily living independently? These ADLs are related to your personal care. Can you bathe yourself? Can you get in and out of a tub or a bed or a chair on your own? Can you walk? Can you take care of yourself toilet-wise? Can you feed yourself?

The second type of health eligibility is the instrumental activities of daily living. Can you prepare your own meals safely? Can you manage your money? Can you do housework? Can you communicate? Can you use a phone?

If a physician declares you deficient in your ADLs, then you need help. You either need an aide to come to your house and help you, or you have to go into a facility.

When you apply for Medicaid, Medicaid will send someone to do an evaluation to determine if you're looking for an aide, how many hours, and the type of aide services you need, or if your condition requires such care that an aide is not enough. In that case, you can apply for facility care.

The Medicaid team will make a decision, not you or your family members, on your behalf. They will determine that you need, say, five hours of care. If they do that, then you only get five hours because Medicaid will only pay for five hours—and tell you where and how that care will be provided. If you need more, you or your family have to pay out of pocket.

Financial Eligibility

Financial eligibility in New York changes from year to year, but as of this year 2024, if you're a single person applying to Medicaid for long-term facility care, you can't have more than $1,732 per month of income.

Income includes Social Security, pension, rental income, and dividends from stocks. They add up all your sources of income. If you make more than $1,732 per month, you are over the income limit for eligibility. If you're married and both of you are applying, it is essentially double, or $2,351 per month.

If you are over the Medicaid income threshold, then you're not eligible for Medicaid.

The income calculation goes deep. If you have whole life insurance, the cash value is calculated, and then they look at your non-IRA accounts, bank accounts, stocks, bonds, and more. They include your investment properties and commercial income. They look at the value of your vacation home. If your IRA is in payout status, the principal is exempt from Medicaid counting it as income. If you pull more money out of an IRA or a qualified retirement account like an annuity, Medicaid is not going to force you to dig into it. It is exempt. There will also never be a Medicaid lien on it (meaning they can seize the assets after your death).

All that will go into their calculation as your assets that make you eligible or not.

Allowable Spend Down for Eligibility

Even if your income qualifies you, you're still not done. Asset evaluation comes next, and that is everything not included in your income and not protected in an appropriate trust (that discussion is coming up).

In short, a single person applying can't have more than $31,176 in assets. If you are married and both of you are applying, your asset limit is $42,318. If you're a married couple and only one of you is applying, the applicant who is applying can't have more than $31,176 in assets. But the non-married non-applicant can have $154,140. Please note that these numbers change at least every year.

To reach that amount, you're allowed to spend your cash in certain ways.

The first is to pay down debt, and doing so may qualify you financially. The spend down has to be real, and paying down verifiable debt is real. If you have a mortgage, a personal or a vehicle loan with an institution (not an informal loan to your daughter or your little brother), or credit card balances—that is real debt. You pay off your debts, thus you've spent down your assets in view to reaching the asset number you need for eligibility for Medicaid services.

In addition to allowed debt pay down, Medicaid has some acceptable expenditures you can use your assets to make. This can include the purchase of medical devices not covered by insurance or home modifications or repairs for accessibility in your elder years (an accessible bathroom, lower cabinets in the kitchen, a wheelchair ramp at the front door, a stairwell lift, the purchase of a handicapped or regular vehicle giving you one car, etc.). You're getting a value for it, plus you're that much closer to getting to the Medicaid threshold amount through accepted spend downs.

Another accepted spend down is irrevocable funeral trusts or prepaid funeral expenses for up to $15,000 per person. In effect, you're paying now for something that you would have to pay for later anyway. It reduces the stress on your survivors because someone has to show up with $15,000. Such prepaid plans move with you from state to state. The other benefit that we saw with prepaid plans was back in the COVID-19 days where the deceased were waiting for burial for some time; people with prepaid plans were taken first.

A prepaid plan won't pay for your cemetery plot, but they will pay for the coffin, the service, opening the ground, and the headstone. They will pay for the wake or whatever is your particular religious service.

There are other acceptable ways to spend down, but those are the main ones that we can use.

That is the financial Medicaid eligibility picture for long-term facility care. Now you see why asset protection planning is crucial if you want to get the health care you need, while still leaving a legacy for your heirs.

Income Solutions

Clearly, if you have only Social Security and a pension as your income, you're never going to get beneath the $1,732 per month income threshold. You would never qualify. So what do you do?

A first solution to look at is the pooled trust, also commonly called "Community Medicaid." This is a trust operated by a charity. If you're making $6,732 a month, you're never going to get below the $1,732 because every month you have your mandatory distribution for your pension and you get Social Security. You're never going to get less. So you keep $1,732, which is the maximum amount for eligibility in your bank account every month, and the $5,000 that you're over the limit goes into this pooled trust, or Community Medicaid.

The charity administers the trust *and* pays for all your costs of living and bills—your rent, food, utilities, trips, insurance—from the funds you have deposited. You have continual use of your $5,000 even when it is in the pooled trust. This simply means you put your money in this pool trust that pays your living expenses.

There is a saying, "He who giveth with the big print taketh away in the small print."

The "giveth" here is that you still have access to that $6,732 from your pension and Social Security. But now, income-wise, you're immediately qualified to get long-term care Medicaid services. And the "taketh away" is that when you pass away, the balance—anything left over in that pooled trust—goes to the charity. Not to your heirs, not the government, but to the charity. I don't consider this a bad thing because typically not much is left over. Remember the pooled trust is paying your bills.

The Look-Back Period

When applying for Medicaid for long-term health care services, the authorities will *look back* at a certain number of years at all your financials and assets. In New York, they take a snapshot of you in the past five years for facility care. They look at all your assets, and they judge you according to your assets.

Those five years they look at is a look-back period that you must plan for. The look-back period for long-term facility care is five years in New York, but for a health aide, it's two and a half years. Note that the length is variable in other states.

Medicaid collects information about all your financials, all your assets. When you provide them with your five-year financials, you have to include how much and when you spent down your debts or made cash or charitable gifts to get to the threshold limits.

If you gave your children $200,000 within the look-back period, Medicaid will assume the purpose of the transfer was to become qualified for Medicaid, and they will count it against you. Any transfer of asset that you make of significance during the look-back period will lead them to assume that you made that to become eligible for Medicaid. All this means is you have to plan far ahead of time. We are attempting to predict your health situation five years into the future.

When you procrastinate about starting the planning, you're doubling your look-back time. If I'm fifty, I'm thinking about a Medicaid plan, but I don't create it. I wait until I'm fifty-two. So I've lost four years—the two from age fifty to fifty-two and the two from age fifty-two to fifty-four. I've doubled my look-back period for my Medicaid eligibility.

Don't wait to plan. Transfers made during the look-back period will be assumed to have been made to become eligible for Medicaid, and while this assumption is challengeable, it is difficult to prove. The best advice is to plan right now and rest easy about your eligibility when you require the care.

The Penalty Period

The next term you will hear is "penalty period." There is a myth around the penalty period. People believe that they will have to pay money to Medicaid. That is, if your assets are over the threshold, now you have to pay Medicaid money. This is not the case.

The penalty period is the amount of time when Medicaid will delay paying for your long-term care needs. Let's say you have $120,000 in cash at the bank, and the average cost for a facility care in your region is $10,000 a month. Medicaid—if you applied right then—will tell you it's going to cost $10,000 a month for your care, and since you have $120,000, talk to them in a year. They're not going to pay for twelve months because you have the money to pay. You're going to have to spend down your cash as a private payer for your medical expenses.

The basic rule here: If you have the assets, don't apply for Medicaid only to be denied.

Remember my single client who had $3 million but all in cash, with no other assets. We are not going to apply for Medicaid to get him denied (and he didn't want that anyway). We are going to shelter whatever assets we can and do the things that you can do to spend down without invoking the penalty period. Once we've gotten you to the point where you're eligible, then you can apply.

We need to carefully examine your eligibility before you apply for Medicaid. But if you only possess a $3 million house that is your primary residence, and you're making $1,000 a month on Social Security and that's all the income you have, you're going to be qualified for Medicaid.

Medicaid will not force you to sell your house. It is a protected asset.[17] Medicaid will not force you to rent your house. Medicaid will not force you to get a loan on your

---

17   In New York State, the first $1,071,000 of equity in your personal home is not counted.

house. You will be qualified for Medicaid. When you pass away, it will not force your spouse to sell your house or get a loan or take a renter to generate income. Medicaid will wait until your spouse passes away, then, because it still has an active lien, Medicaid comes around to collect when you and your spouse have passed. That is so, unless you have planned and protected your assets well in advance.

Like it or not, remember the goal is to have the government pay for your medical expenses. We don't want to use our own money for our medical expenses but prefer to have the government pay.

Your goal is to preserve your assets, preserve your legacy, and use your money the way you choose to during your lifetime.

Your First Line of Defense: Long-Term Care Insurance

Before we get into a valuable trust for long-term Medicaid planning (coming in the next chapter), there is what I call your "first line of defense." It is a long-term care insurance policy.

Long-term care insurance is the first line of defense in preparing for long-term health care costs as the least restrictive to you. It provides coverage for in-home care, assisted living, and residential nursing home care.

There are two basic types of long-term care insurance. There is "traditional long-term care insurance," which is like car insurance. You pay a premium every month. If you don't get hit by a car, then there is no payout to you. If you get hit by a car, then there is a payout. If you need it, it's there. If not, you're just paying the premium. Traditional long-term care premiums can go up the older you get, and they could even drop later on. Alas, this is exactly what we see with auto insurance and home insurance too.

The second type is what we call a "hybrid whole life insurance policy." This is a whole life insurance policy that has an endorsement (also called a "rider," which changes or adds to the policy in a specific manner) for long-term care. The benefit is if you never go on long-term care, your beneficiaries get the death benefit. You're paying a premium, and regardless of what happens, there is a payout, in this case, to your beneficiaries.

Now, if you're deficient in your ADLs, and you need long-term care, the endorsement of your policy comes to life and pays for your care, depending on the amounts and services your policy covers. The payment eats away at the death benefit.

Your hybrid policy will have a higher premium than your traditional LTC insurance, but your premiums are static. They never go up, and they never expire. They can't drop you once you sign up for it. A lot of people prefer the hybrid, even though it is more expensive, for just those reasons.

Beware Deductibles

I have a client who had a traditional long-term care policy with cheap premiums—at the expense of home care. She had a $40,000 home care deductible, which you might agree was huge. Keep in mind that most people want home health aides to come to the house and avoid going into a facility. But if you have a $40,000 deductible (and whether you see it as a huge deductible or not), is that to your advantage? You have to first spend your own $40,000 for the aide, and then coverage kicks in. Always ask what the deductibles are for the various services covered.

For legitimate caregivers who provide twelve hours of care, you're looking at anything from $350 to $500 a day, or from $6,000 to $15,000 per month. Most of these policies are written per day, so you can go for less than that amount. Remember that if your policy covers $250 per day, and it's costing you $350, you have to kick in the extra $100 out of your pocket.

If you bring in someone "cheaper," you're asking for trouble. If it's your neighbor from church or the son of a friend—are they trained and qualified? Probably not. If they're moving Dad from the bed to the chair, and they drop him, and the chair falls on the caregiver's leg and breaks it, guess what? You get sued. If you put them on the books, and you pay for payroll and you pay for workers' compensation, they're covered by workers' comp. Also, if you pay for it on the books, you get the deduction, whereas you can't deduct a cash person. When you consider your liability, it is endless, so beware and be aware of the potential risks.

Now, I said that long-term care insurance is the first line of defense. Let me modify that a bit and say that it is an important component of a full-on health care and asset protection strategy. The cornerstone of the strategy is a specific type of irrevocable trust. Let's look at it now.

CHAPTER 11

Medicaid Asset Protection Trust

Health is not valued till sickness comes.
—Thomas Fuller

We talked about the concept of Medicaid asset protection and the benefits of it, but not how to implement such a thing. That brings us to a discussion of a specific type of irrevocable trust, the Medicaid Asset Protection Trust (MAPT).

Remember the commonality of irrevocable trusts: These trusts avoid probate. It is difficult, if not impossible, to amend them. Thus, I encourage all my clients to think deeply about why they want to create them and with which assets they wish to fund such trusts. You will also see why it is important to fund this trust all at once and right away—after discussing and thinking it through with an experienced estate and tax attorney like me.

This trust strategy has a dual benefit: (1) A MAPT will allow you to qualify for long-term care through Medicaid, and (2) a MAPT allows your legacy to go to your heirs and not have to be spent paying for long-term health care. The purpose of this trust is to protect assets from Medicaid's long-term care income and asset evaluation. Remember how you qualify for Medicaid—with low asset and income amounts.

You can fund a MAPT with any type of asset, except for IRAs. Why not an IRA? It is an *individual* retirement account, and a trust is not an individual. You can fund a MAPT with personal property (like cash bank accounts), real property (like buildings or residences), securities, and annuities.

The MAPT must be understood before you fund it: The person who receives the benefit isn't you as the grantor or creator of this trust. It's really for the benefit of your beneficiaries. That is the first consideration.

Second, a MAPT also protects your assets from Medicaid liens. Create this trust to ensure inheritance by avoiding having Medicaid place a lien on the asset. After the look-back period expires, Medicaid can't seek reimbursement for any asset you put in. You have to think about a Medicaid trust as a lockbox. What you put into it stays inside.

Third, after the look-back period expires, whatever is in the MAPT is invisible and therefore not counted as your asset when it comes to Medicaid's calculations to determine what the penalty period is or what you have to spend down.

As always, I will have had in-depth discussions with you about your needs, goals, assets, and decisions about who you leave what assets to upon your death.

Going back to my clients with the brownstone, we put their brownstone and $300,000 cash inside a MAPT (because the minimum amount they want to leave each of their three children is $100,000). Outside of the MAPT, we created a revocable trust for their remaining assets, and they purchased long-term care insurance.

They had $300,000 of cash assets in the revocable trust to do whatever they wanted to do with—go on vacation, buy cars, give money as gifts. They paid their bills without any interruption to their regular everyday living. After five years, the brownstone and cash in the MAPT became exempt from Medicaid's reimbursement or asset calculation—and that period is important to understand. That period is why you need such a plan now and not later. Later is too late.

When a MAPT is done timely, the brownstone house and cash in the trust doesn't enter into consideration as part of your income or assets in the eyes of Medicaid. Medicaid can't come after that house after you pass away. That $300,000 inside your MAPT is likewise protected from seizure by the Medicaid authorities. You can go to bed at night knowing your kids are going to have unfettered access to that cash and the brownstone without having to worry about a Medicaid situation on the outside.

If you never go through the other $300,000 in that revocable trust at any point in time because you have been comfortably living off the income from your IRAs, pensions, Social Security, and other investments, then you have that $300,000 in your back pocket to do whatever you want with. Live the good life, knowing that should one or both of you need assistance and need to go on Medicaid, you have that cushion.

With both the MAPT and the revocable trust, you avoid probate and get to do all the wonderful things that a revocable trust does, which we spoke about in prior chapters. By having a long-term care insurance policy, you're double- and triple-backed up financially and medically for yourself and for your legacy to your heirs. Medicaid sees only the assets that you want them to see, and your legacy is preserved for your heirs.

Thus, as in this example, you might have a net worth of $3.5–$4 million and still rest easy that you and your legacy are covered all around—and that you're also eligible to access long-term medical assistance in the process.

This planning necessitates thinking about your wishes years in advance of needing any long-term care because of the Medicaid clock running to what is called the "look-back period." That's a gamble, since none of us knows what the future holds for our health. That's why now is the best time to understand Medicaid and long-term health care, do this planning, implement it, and let the clock run.

The Look-Back Period

Planning enough years ahead for the MAPT and its funding with your assets is crucial because of the look-back period that Medicaid has on any asset protection measures you take.

Any asset you have funded the trust with—placed in the trust—is "invisible" after five years as far as Medicaid is concerned. Medicaid doesn't use it as a countable asset when it looks at your eligibility for Medicaid. If you have placed, for example, your vacation home in the MAPT, starting five years after you've transferred it into the trust, Medicaid may not put a lien on that property. Remember that a lien ensures that Medicaid, after your death, can come after the vacation home and sell it to pay itself back for all the long-term care you have received "on the house." Also remember that if you have only your primary residence in the MAPT, it is exempt from Medicaid's accounting.

The Step-Up in Basis Adjustment

First, what is that "basis adjustment," or "step-up in basis," and why is it important for assets in your trusts?

Step-up in basis is a tax provision that adjusts the cost basis of an inherited asset to its fair market value on the date of the previous owner's death—upon your death if you're the one who created the trust. When someone inherits an asset, such as stocks, real estate, or other investments, the cost basis of that asset is "stepped up" to its current market value at the time of the owner's death. This effectively eliminates any capital gains that occurred during the deceased person's ownership of the asset.[18]

Here's the rub: The IRS passed Revenue Rule 2023-2, which determined an irrevocable trust doesn't qualify for that step-up and that elimination of capital gains tax. That's bad news for the beneficiary, I think you can agree.

Here's the solution: Proper drafting of your MAPT.

The law says that any asset in the MAPT is no longer your asset. You lose control over those assets, and the assets can't be used in any way for your benefit.

Uncle Sam will give in the big print and take away in the fine print. One aspect of that fine print regards "a basis adjustment" for assets in an irrevocable trust like the

---

18   "Step-Up in Basis," Tax Foundation, accessed November 9, 2024, https://taxfoundation.org/taxedu/glossary/step-up-in-basis/.

MAPT. The default rule for the IRS is you don't get a basis adjustment on assets in a MAPT or any irrevocable trust unless you plan correctly.

We have to put particular language in your irrevocable trust to make sure your heirs and the assets benefit from a basis adjustment upon your death, if it's appropriate for you. We run some formulas to see if it makes sense for you to give up a basis adjustment to save inheritance tax.

Because there is a limited to no ability to amend an irrevocable trust's terms, you again need to deeply consider the purpose of the trust, the assets you fund it with, and the beneficiaries inheriting down the line.

There is a loss of control. You're not the trustee. You're not the owner of the assets, so they can't be used by you to your benefit. If you put $100,000 cash into a Medicaid Asset Protection Trust, and you want to take a trip to Disneyland or you need to buy a car, you can't go to your trustee and say, "Buy me that Mercedes from the trust money."

Say that you funded the MAPT with $100,000 in cash that is invested in dividend-producing stocks. The principal can't come out but the dividend income comes to you. Same if you funded the trust with an income-generating piece of real estate, you benefit only from the net income of the real estate for your costs of living and expenses. You don't typically keep that income accruing inside the MAPT.

To remain in compliance with the rules, the principal doesn't come out of a Medicaid trust, but income generated from it can. If the principal comes out to your benefit,

Medicaid is going to say it is noncompliant. The Medicaid trust is specifically designed to cut the strings of ownership.

I like my clients to understand the rules—that fine print—up front. I've had clients come in with a MAPT. They've taken $10,000 from the trust and gifted it to the son, and then on the back end, the son gives them $5,000 of that $10,000. That's an illegal manipulation of trust assets. Medicaid can look at that as being noncompliant, and you've wasted the time and money to set up that MAPT. You've lost the time you were building up toward the five-year look-back period. You don't want to play fast and loose for short-term benefits.

Putting assets in the MAPT must be thoughtfully done with a mind to your daily expenses and costs of living so that assets you need to cover your costs of living aren't locked away and unavailable to you. We look at what your cash flow is to make sure you can still live a good life, a happy life, and if this asset was removed from your portfolio or from whatever you own, we want to make sure that you're not destitute. You want to organize your finances so that you can still, for example, pay property taxes or the lawn guy, pay for regular repair and maintenance of your home or vehicle, or fund your annual travel.

With patience, you reap the big benefit of the MAPT. When I have a client whose sole or primary asset that they want to pass down to their children is the house, then a

MAPT is an effective strategy to ensure that the house goes to the kids while you still keep the potential income from it.

What about flexibility? You know irrevocable trusts are "carved in stone." Say that your New York house is in your MAPT, and you're six years into the MAPT. The look-back period is fulfilled. The house is valued at $1 million. What if you decide to move out of state? You could sell the house that is within the MAPT through the trustee. The net proceeds of sale would have to remain in the trust. It doesn't come out to you.

That $1 million that you got from the sale of the house is now part of the MAPT. You can't take a dime or a dollar of that by saying you want $10,000 or $150,000 of that in cash for your pocket. You can, however, use some or all of that $1 million to buy a new house in Utah or South Dakota or Louisiana. You just make sure that the new house is purchased in the name of the trust. The owner of that house is, like the one you sold, the MAPT. Even if you buy a $500,000 home with half of the $1 million you have, you now have $500,000 of value in a home and $500,000 in cash—both owned by the MAPT. That cash can't be used to your benefit.

A bonus to you is this: The sale of the house doesn't spark a new look-back period because the funds from the sale are still in control of the trust. The asset merely changed species or form—from real property to cash, then to more real property.

Bulletproof?

All the strategies we have discussed so far in the context of long-term health care protection—the MAPT, the irrevocable trust, the long-term care insurance policy on at least one of the couple—when taken together, make you about as bulletproof as you can get from a health care, financial, tax, and legacy-protection perspective.

The Cadillac plan:

- An irrevocable trust (MAPT)
- A revocable trust
- A long-term care insurance policy

Long-Term Care Insurance: Whom to Insure?

Let's briefly revisit our long-term care insurance strategy. What is the rationale for a married couple for getting the insurance on one rather than on both of you?

First, it is insurance, and there is a health exam attached to qualification for coverage. We don't know if both of you can qualify. If one can't be covered for health reasons, we get coverage for the other spouse. Also, if you both apply and qualify, we can decide to cover the one with the lowest quoted premium for the most amount of coverage possible. It's a "spend with a purpose" approach.

Now one person has long-term care insurance. If that person needs long-term care, they have the insurance and the insurance will pay. Long-term care insurance not only pays for your long-term care but gives you time to make adjustments to plan for the other person.

You do this ideally while neither of you needs or has applied for Medicaid. Remember the look-back period. Five years is a long time when you consider health issues with need for care usually being immediate and pressing. With three or four years of payments through a long-term care insurance plan, you now have that much planning time to create, fund, and fulfill your MAPT's look-back period.

A couple will take care to transfer the assets if there are joint accounts over to the person with the insurance policy (who will not require or apply, in other words, for Medicaid). Another aspect of this is there is no look-back period for interspousal transfers. Now, any time the spouse without the insurance policy needs care, they will be Medicaid-eligible.

Spousal Refusal

"Spousal refusal" is a Medicaid planning strategy that allows the spouse of a Medicaid applicant to refuse to contribute their income or assets toward the cost of the applicant's long-term care. You see right away that it would be the spouse with the long-term care insurance policy who will be exercising the spousal refusal, which is based in federal Medicaid law.

The law states that Medicaid can't deny coverage to an eligible individual solely because their spouse refuses to provide financial support. This provision is part of the "anti-spousal impoverishment laws" enacted in the late 1980s to protect community spouses from financial ruin. As I write this, New York is one the few states that actively allow and recognize spousal refusal.[19] This is a strategy you need to discuss in all cases with an attorney familiar with the law, as there are documents to file, assets to protect, and time needed to implement it.

The state offices of Medicaid can still attempt to seek reimbursement even after the spousal refusal, and in that case, we typically negotiate with Medicaid to limit or have them agree not to go after the spouse. Medicaid typically will not agree to a zero-dollar settlement, but if assets are a house or cash money that you require to live on, Medicaid may agree to limit what they would want reimbursement for. It does mitigate the spousal refusal reimbursement potential. This mitigation of the spousal refusal strategy is why having long-term care insurance is advantageous.

To wrap up Medicaid Asset Protection Trusts, I need to repeat myself:

- You are not benefiting from the MAPT—your heirs are. You're only benefiting in the sense that you're protecting your assets from going to your long-term Medicaid costs instead of to your designated heirs.

---

19   Jack Halpern, "Spousal Refusal for Medicaid Eligibility: Just Being Mean or Financial Survival?" My Elder, accessed November 9, 2024, https://myelder.com/spousal-refusal-for-medicaid-eligibility-just-being-mean-or-financial-survival/.

- You're making sure these assets go to your heirs without having to worry about coming out of pocket for your long-term care in any way. You want to have Medicaid pay for your long-term care needs.

- You can no longer use the principal of assets in the trust, so the assets you put in the trust must not affect your daily cash flow needs. You can only access and spend the income an asset in the MAPT generates.

- You have no ability or limited ability to amend the trust or remove assets once they are in the trust.

- You make yourself bulletproof as regards long-term health care costs and Medicaid rules by combining the MAPT with a revocable trust and appropriate long-term care insurance.

A word of caution: Don't just *create* the irrevocable MAPT—*fund* it immediately and fully as well. Good planning includes implementation of the MAPT. Signing a trust into existence is no good to you—nor will it start the look-back period clock—unless you fund it with all the assets you have determined need protection. Funding the trust immediately triggers the look-back period clock on the date you funded the trust with that particular asset or set of assets.

You should consider your MAPT as soon as possible because no one can tell when they're going to need care. When considering your plan, we'll look at your big picture, then at the details specific to you, and fund the MAPT fully all at once. That way, you know exactly when the look-back period has been fulfilled without delay or guesswork.

Having an experienced attorney like me advising you is key. I will correctly examine your cash flow needs, your assets, and your legacy wishes. I will help you gain a clear understanding of the look-back period and its risks and its advantages to you and your qualification for long-term care insurance coverage, not to mention the tax implications for you across these topics. There are plenty of attorneys out there who will draft up the trust for you but won't give you the proper advice and guidance or won't assist you in transferring the assets.

PART 3

Build a Wall Around Your Beneficiaries

Parents always want to do the right thing, but passing down wealth without a plan can sometimes bestow burdens instead of blessings.
—Stephen Bonfa

I help adult clients deal with crises with their elder parents. I see people of all ages and help them plan for their own future, retirement needs, and legacy goals. I also find myself helping clients plan for the future of loved ones in the next younger generation—their children.

Every generation might hold beneficiaries, family, and other loved ones that you wish to include in your legacy. Sometimes we need to build a wall around vulnerable beneficiaries—and here, I mean a wall that Uncle Sam can't breach. Thus, as a key part of my estate planning conversation, I will try to know the story of your chosen beneficiaries, family members, and heirs.

This is not just me making conversation or being nosy, although I could tell you some stories that will put hair on your teeth. We need to uncover any special accommodation your beneficiaries are enjoying and include these concerns in our plans to ensure they will continue on without interruption.

A big part of planning—tax planning and the "who gets what" of estate planning—is understanding the impact of your plan on the beneficiary and customizing your plan to benefit them as much as possible.

CHAPTER 12

Supplemental Needs Trust

*Disability should never disqualify anyone from
accessing every aspect of life.*
—Emma Thompson

Clients of mine have children or beneficiaries with a disability or some special need that will stay with them throughout their lives. We need to be concerned about how to protect those beneficiaries' well-being—whatever the situation.

A Supplemental Needs Trust (SNT) is a tool we can use in certain situations. It is a specialized legal arrangement designed to improve the quality of life for individuals with disabilities while preserving their eligibility for needs-based government benefits such as Medicaid, Supplemental Security Income (SSI), housing assistance, or other programs that make their lives more comfortable.

In short, if you have a beneficiary on government assistance, you want to build extra protection around them when you add them as beneficiaries of any kind to your plan.

This could be your own child, another family member, a friend, or any beneficiary who has a disability. The disability might be developmental (such as autism or a physical birth defect) or purely accidental (they get hit by a bus, lose an arm or an eye, or become paralyzed).

If that person is getting any needs-based governmental assistance, you can both (1) give them an inheritance and (2) protect and preserve their needs-based assistance with proper planning.

If Section 8 Housing[20] has an income limit, and your beneficiary inherits $100,000 from you, it will push them over the established asset limit. Suddenly, with no Section 8, they lose their place to live. Perhaps their doctors or the care facility where they're getting certain services are income-based, and now they have to pay cash out of pocket for their care and perhaps for their doctor visits.

---

20   Section 8 Housing, or the Housing Choice Voucher Program, is a federally funded initiative assisting with housing for low-income families, the elderly, and individuals with disabilities. "Section 8 Housing," USA.gov, accessed February 19, 2025, https://www.usa.gov/housing-voucher-section-8.

If you gave them money outright, their inheritance can put them over the income or asset limit for program eligibility and cause them to lose their health care, housing, or other assistance. What then? Instead of being able to enjoy the inheritance, they're going to have to waste your inheritance to pay for their essential services—that they were getting for free—and disrupt their life. Soon, the inheritance money is gone, and they must go through the whole process of reapplying for assistance.

I had a gentleman the other day tell me he waited three years to get approved for SSI benefits. It was his first application. Reapplying can likewise be a long, long process—and during that wait, your beneficiary will need care and services.

You want to and can avoid that happening to your heirs. Financial eligibility requirements are strict for government programs. For most programs, if you're a dollar over the asset/income limit, services can be terminated.

The third-party (i.e., not funded by the beneficiary) Supplemental Needs Trust is designed to allow a disabled person on government assistance to stay on their assistance. It *supplements* it. The SNT essentially becomes invisible to the eligibility restrictions. The SNT allows your disabled beneficiary to inherit 100 percent of their inheritance because, as its name suggests, it *supplements* what they're getting from government assistance.

If you have someone who fits this situation—has a disability and is getting financial-based services—it is imperative that you create a SNT for that person. Then the inheritance to them goes through the SNT.

You may not have an heir who is disabled when you create your estate plan. But you never know what can happen in life. Perhaps your future grandchild is born with autism or your cousin gets into a debilitating accident. You can prepare for this possibility now. I call this provision "in case of emergency, break glass," because you may never need it.

If you included a SNT in your estate plan, but no one needs it, the provision is just words on a page. But if some unfortunate event occurs, that SNT is a lifesaver. You break that glass, and the SNT is created.

Having a SNT will avoid a very real, harsh impact on your beneficiary. Don't jeopardize that child who is getting services because they have a disability. Your plan should include a Supplemental Needs Trust.

The SNT could pay for the following things, without jeopardizing your heir's assistance: companionship, rent, or food, as well as fixing the house, taking a vacation, and paying for transport assistance, wheelchair, and such.

In other words, the funds can supplement what they're getting on government assistance without losing government assistance.

Special Needs or Supplemental Needs?

Oftentimes uninformed people use the terms "special needs trusts" and "Supplemental Needs Trusts" interchangeably. There is a real distinction between these two terms. One is a "third-party" trust (Supplemental Needs) and the other is a "first-party" trust (special needs).

Imagine you're a disabled person, and you have money. You have some assets. You can create a first-party special needs trust. You're funding, or putting your money, into the trust. An important fact with the first-party special needs trust is that when you pass away, the government can seek reimbursement from the trust assets. The authorities can put a lien on the first-party special needs trust and collect from the trust what the agencies spent on disability services for you over your lifetime.

When you provide for your loved one with a Supplemental Needs Trust, this is a third-party trust. Someone else—grandparents, benefactors—is funding the trust with their money. Unlike the first-party special needs trust, when the disabled beneficiary passes away with a third-party Supplemental Needs Trust, the government can't seek reimbursement for its services from the trust. You can direct where the remainder goes.

Let's say you create a third-party Supplemental Needs Trust for your two kids, only one of whom has a disability right now and is currently getting assistance. The trust beneficiary is the disabled child. You can state that when that disabled child passes away, the remainder goes to the other child or to someone else entirely. You choose who it goes to. But the bottom line is that Uncle Sam stays out of your pockets.

Remember my prior comments about using the correct language in your estate documents? Some unsophisticated lawyers who don't understand the difference and identify the trust as a special needs trust instead of a Supplement Needs Trust can cause some governmental agencies to consider it a first-party trust from which they can seek reimbursement. While your heirs may end up convincing the agency otherwise, they will often have to appeal the agency's determination. This will cause delays and additional expense.

It is imperative that the terms special needs trust and Supplemental Needs Trust are not confused or used interchangeably in your estate plan. If the trust is misidentified, well, Medicaid and Social Security have been known to fight you (the estate) because they want reimbursement—all because your misinformed attorney has labeled your trust incorrectly.

CHAPTER 13

IRA Provisions for Beneficiary Protections and Taxes, Taxes, Taxes!

I'm proud to pay taxes in the United States; the only thing is, I could be just as proud for half the money.
—Comedian Arthur Godfrey

Most of my clients have IRAs. Whether it's a traditional IRA or Roth IRA that you created and have been funding, you probably intended it to supplement your Social Security benefits. Everyone knows that we can't live on Social

Security benefits alone, and that was not the goal of the program in the first place.

During your lifetime, you created and contributed a portion of your income into an IRA and, depending on the type of IRA you opened, the tax benefits to you are variable. You must take the required mandatory distributions in the year you turn seventy-three. It is not my purpose here to discuss when or how much to withdraw from your IRAs, but rather to show you how to protect your named beneficiaries from as much taxation as possible when they inherit your IRA account.

Most people know to list beneficiaries on their IRAs because they don't want their IRA beneficiaries to go through a probate proceeding before getting the IRA distribution. Your IRA will give, say, everything to your wife, and then if your wife isn't alive, you leave everything to your children equally. That's a typical plain vanilla beneficiary designation.

The Custodial Letter

The problem with IRAs is that when you pass away, your heir will get a letter from the IRA custodian (the institution holding your account) that reads something like, "You have $500,000 of an IRA that you're inheriting from so-and-so. Sign here _____." The letter will ask how much your heir wants to withhold for taxes, and then send them a check for what's left.

Remember that I'm here to advise you (and thus your heirs) on how to pay only your fair share of taxes and not a

nickel more to Uncle Sam. To that end, I am informing you, the IRA owner, and your heir of the IRA of some crucial information. Read my next words carefully:

Taking a lump sum payment has put your heir in the worst possible tax position.

Now, understand that the IRA custodian has no obligation to be anyone's tax advisor. They explicitly say they are not giving tax advice and tell you to seek professional tax advice. While the big print announces, "Hey, you're inheriting thousands of dollars from so-and-so," we must remember the fine print in that hidden paragraph. It states, "We're not giving you tax advice."

The reason why taking an IRA inheritance in a lump sum puts your heir in the worst possible tax position is that it may cost them 40 percent or more in taxes. Yes, your heir could lose half the money that you sacrificed to save and grow in that IRA. Half!

Let me put some real numbers on this to show you how this tragedy unfolds. Let's say your IRA has $500,000 in it. When you pass, your (uninformed) beneficiary will sign that custodial letter, agreeing to withhold 30 percent for taxes, and then get the lump sum payout, because, hey, someone said always take the lump sum when you win the lotto.

Your beneficiary's 30 percent is $150,000. For taxes. Now they get a check for the remaining $350,000 (and not the $500,000 that the account held). They deposit it in their bank account and then, as most people will do, use that money right away to improve their house, buy a new car, pay off bills, or take an amazing vacation.

Then, the following April at tax time, they file their taxes and boom! They now have to declare whatever income they earned that year plus an additional $500,000 (the gross amount inherited) in income. They forgot that this bequest amount comes in addition to all their other usual income. This pushes them from their usual 22 percent tax bracket into the 35 percent tax bracket.

The increase in income could very well result in the beneficiary losing 40 percent of the bequest to taxes.

Don't despair. And don't stop reading.

The Solution: The Inherited IRA

I'm all about mitigating or eliminating taxes in all the allowed ways, as you know by now. To achieve that mitigation, the heir can create what we call an "inherited IRA," or "beneficiary IRA."

This means that you as owner of the IRA should inform your beneficiary that this solution exists.

Here's what to do. Instead of taking that "default" lump sum that the custodian presumptively announced, an inherited IRA is created by your heirs after your death through your financial planner. Instead of getting a lump sum in a single check as discussed above, the whole IRA amount of $500,000 rolls into the inherited IRA your heir created.

- If it was a traditional IRA, when the heir pulls money from the inherited IRA, it is taxed at the personal income tax rate the year the beneficiary withdrew the money.

- If it was a Roth IRA, it is generally (but again there are rules) tax-free to the beneficiary at withdrawal time.

Next, let's look at the detailed withdrawal and tax picture.

Your Tax Picture and the Secure Act 2.0

Once upon a time, if you inherited IRA funds and your life expectancy was fifty years, you *could have* stretched those IRA distributions over your lifetime by rolling the IRA into an inherited IRA. Instead of getting $500,000 in one year, you would have taken it out in equal increments for your remaining fifty-year lifetime. That would be $10,000 per year (in addition to whatever gains the investments in the account made) and that amount would have a small, and perhaps zero, impact on most people's tax bracket.

Things are different today because of—you guessed it—Congress.

Earlier, I emphasized *could have* stretched over fifty years. But when the US Congress passed the Secure Act 2.0 on December 29, 2022, our ability to stretch the withdrawals for more than ten years for certain beneficiaries was limited. That $500,000 IRA taken in the recommended equal amounts each year means you have $50,000 more in taxable income for ten years now. That may change your tax bracket but still be less than a lump sum distribution.

Now, however, you have some new information about inherited IRAs—whether you're the benefactor or the beneficiary.

I can't repeat this enough:

Inform your beneficiary about the inherited IRA.

Your beneficiary can roll your IRA distribution into an inherited IRA. By opting for this, your beneficiary can spread their payments over ten or more years (depending on their relationship to you). This minimizes the amount of income received per year and minimizes the nightmare of that jump into a higher tax bracket.

Also keep in mind that if your IRA proceeds become probate property, it will pour into the estate. If the IRA is liquidated into the estate, it will be a taxable event. The Secure Act 2.0 allows the transfer of one IRA into an inherited IRA and *stretching* the withdrawals over the course of ten years and reduce the tax impact.

The Inherited IRA Trust

Remember that the strategy I just described depends on your beneficiaries knowing about the impending tax cliff and knowing they need to create the inherited IRA. There is another way to inform them and protect your heirs' tax picture.

What if I told you that you can mandate in your estate plan that your beneficiary must roll over their IRA distribution into their own inherited IRA—or at least has to get tax advice before making a decision.

You can form an inherited IRA trust, and the trustee of your choosing can ensure that your beneficiaries get the most of your money possible. You would instruct your trustee to create, when you pass away, an inherited IRA and stretch out the payments. Alternatively, if the beneficiary is in real financial need, the trustee can allow a lump sum payment.

This important IRA planning strategy removes the initial knee-jerk agreement by the unsuspecting beneficiary to collect the lump sum, only to be hit with a giant tax bill. Much as a minor's trust is a buffer (see chapter 15), so is this inherited IRA trust.

By incorporating inherited IRA trust planning into your estate plan, you can ensure that your beneficiaries make an informed and educated decision to choose either stretching their payments over time or taking a one-time lump sum distribution. You can use the IRS's rules to your favor.

This trust can avoid the panic I witnessed with a client beneficiary. During our regularly scheduled tax strategy meeting, she quite offhandedly mentioned that her father had died, and she just got a $400,000 check.

My client told me she signed the papers for the IRA lump sum payout.

Had she spoken to me first, I would have extolled the virtues of rolling the IRA proceeds into an inherited IRA. Instead, after I did some guesstimate tax math, I had to tell her that with a stroke of her pen, she now owed $120,000 in income taxes. She would have to pay the equivalent of a down payment on a house (as she put it) to Uncle Sam. She was panicked, then distraught.

I reluctantly had to tell her that, unlike a distribution for your own IRA where you have sixty days to roll it over into another IRA, once the distribution is made to a beneficiary because of the death of the owner, there is no turning back. She did not have sixty days, not thirty days, not even two hours to roll the distribution into an inherited IRA. It needed to be paid from the IRA into an inherited IRA, never having entered into her pockets.

After picking her jaw up off the floor, she muttered that she had received the check that day and was on the way to the bank to cash it. A wave of relief washed over me—the check was not yet cashed. I immediately jumped into action. I was able to get the IRA custodian to cancel the check and re-issue the funds directly to an inherited IRA. By a stroke of luck, quick thinking, some speed dialing (and no small degree of persuasion), I was able to grab over $110,000 from Uncle Sam's hands and put it back into my client's pocket.

That is the value of an inherited IRA trust—and having a top-notch tax attorney who knows tax law.

CHAPTER 14

Addiction Protection for Heirs

Fall seven times, get up eight.
—Japanese proverb

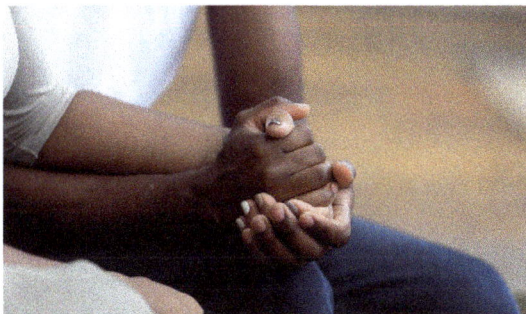

In this brief chapter, I might write the words "addiction" or "substance abuse" or refer to drugs or alcohol, but I know as well as you do that there are many types of addictions that can threaten the well-being and decision-making power of any person, as well as tempt the individual to spend, spend, spend to feed the addiction. So keep that in mind as you read this section, please.

Watching a loved one struggle with addiction is difficult enough, but more than a few struggle in silence without you knowing a thing about it. You don't want to give cash, your house, or other assets to someone who's struggling with addiction—and it's not because you're judging them for their behaviors. Not at all. It's just that, while they're in the throes of their addiction, they could go through any amount of money you leave to them so fast it could endanger their health or put them in a graver material circumstance when the money is gone than before they had it.

Also, it is true: You work all your life to own a house and save money, and now the person who's being unfortunately controlled by their addiction has money that they can spend all at once. They have a house that they could sell or take out a mortgage on, or they don't make the remaining mortgage payments and lose the property. They then lose your house to their addiction.

If you have someone who's going through this hardship and struggle, or a loved one suffering alone and in secret, you don't want to make their situation worse.

Your family member or beneficiary with the issue could be someone you already know has the addiction. But if you're providing for your currently minor child, you don't know if your healthy and happy ten-year-old son or daughter will remain so throughout their life. You don't know how their life is going to go, what choices they might make, or what lifestyle they might get trapped into later in childhood or as an adult.

You want to protect them from themselves and ensure their inheritance is there to help them.

A Drug and Alcohol Provision

Remember when I spoke about provisions in trusts that are "in case of emergency, break glass"? Potential drug or alcohol abuse is one of those cases where you're providing for something that may or may not occur—a change in lifestyle, health, wellness, and decision-making power—and you do it with protecting the heir (and the bequest) in mind.

> ### Drug and Alcohol Provision
>
> A drug and alcohol provision ensures the long-term welfare and financial stability of beneficiaries who may be struggling with substance abuse issues.
>
> - The provision is designed to protect the assets from potential misuse by stipulating that beneficiaries must meet certain conditions related to sobriety or participation in rehabilitation programs before they can access their inheritance.
> - The provision safeguards the assets from being squandered but also encourages beneficiaries to pursue a healthier lifestyle.

A drug and alcohol or addiction provision can either be specific to the person (e.g., John or Julie) or to the trust (e.g., the Supplemental Needs Trust or the inherited IRA trust). If you have healthy beneficiaries at the time you wrote your plan, several things can transpire. First, they remain healthy. Second, they develop the addiction, but during your lifetime you weren't aware of it. Third, you know during your lifetime that they are already struggling with addiction. You can provide protection in all those cases. Your executor or trustee can break that glass as needed because you've provided for that.

This provision allows your trustee or executor to take a look at what's going on. If they reasonably believe that an heir is struggling with addiction, they can force that person to take a test to verify it or oblige that person to participate in rehabilitation programs before they can get the money and assets. The trustee can also determine that the heir will get the money either outright in a lump sum or paid out to them over the course of time.

Again, this provision acts as a buffer between the person suffering with substance abuse and the inheritance that may further sink them into the addiction. You set up your provision so the addiction doesn't lead them to further deplete their health and well-being by funding the addiction with their inheritance. Such a provision also encourages them to maintain a clean life, because otherwise the inheritance will be out of their reach.

I had a client who came to me for his estate plan. He told me that his father died, and unbeknownst to him or his father, his brother was suffering and struggling with addiction.

When you have no plan, no trust, no will, you recall that this is called "dying intestate." The brother inherited a lump sum of $50,000 in an account along with a house from his deceased father. The house became the brother's party house, then his drug house. The brother went through the $50,000 cash and stopped paying the property taxes. The brother never even thought to sell the house for more money; he just lived in the house until he couldn't. He couldn't, because the state came in and foreclosed on a tax lien and on the defaulted mortgage. The state took this $800,000 house in Queens, and his brother is now homeless and no one knows where, or even if, he is living.

The client recounting this unfortunate turn of events had young children. He got quite emotional as he expressed that he never wanted this to happen to his children. He was overjoyed when I explained we could add a provision in his trust that, while it could not heal any addiction, could protect and hold an inheritance for when the struggling heir recovers.

You don't have a crystal ball. Sh*t happens. And that's why you must have a plan—provisions in your will and trust documents that allow struggling heirs to have some assets but not lose themselves along the way.

CHAPTER 15

Minor's Trust—They Can't Inherit, So . . . ?

Adults devise a plan and follow it.
Children do what feels good.
—Dave Ramsey

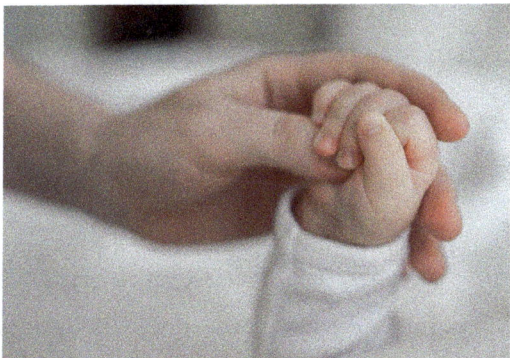

As a professional advisor and as a father, I speak to my clients who are parents of minor children or disabled children (both minor and adult) about caring for their offspring should anything happen to them.

To finish Dave Ramsey's thought: You need a plan for your minor children. Let's look at what you can do, beyond our previous discussion in chapter 12 about protecting special needs or supplemental needs through those types of trusts.

A Minor's Trust

- Allows a grantor to set aside assets for the benefit of a minor beneficiary
- Safeguards the assets until the beneficiary reaches an age specified in the will or trust agreement
- States how the funds can be used, typically according to ascertainable standards, for the minor's health, education, maintenance, and support
- Establishes a "buffer" between the minor and their inheritance

Protecting Assets for Minor Children

We read too many stories in the press about accidental deaths of parents with minor children with no legal, well-designed plan in place to take on the care of their surviving children.

Some of my clients state, "I have a robust life insurance policy for them; they're covered." Yes and no.

New York State considers anyone under the age of eighteen to be a minor.[21] In most states, if you're under the age of eighteen, you can't own assets outright. Minors can't collect inherited assets either. Once a person turns eighteen, they've legally reached the age of majority. Once the age of majority is attained, an individual is legally an adult and may enter into contracts, own property, and manage their own financial affairs.

But pause here and think about when you were eighteen. What would you have done back then if you had suddenly come into $100,000 or several million dollars and no supervision? I know what I would have done. Party, cars, no thoughts about the future, and fun, fun, fun! But, alas, only until the accounts are empty. Then the party's over.

My point is that an eighteen-year-old has virtually no life experience and, in today's culture, little to no education in how to manage money. That is why planning now is so important and why I include a minor's trust in every one of my estate plans.

A minor's trust is typically established by parents, grandparents, or other relatives who want to leave property or assets to a minor child while ensuring responsible management until the child is old enough to handle the inheritance independently.

You can set up this trust or include provisions in your will that delay the distribution of assets until the beneficiary reaches a certain age, such as twenty-one or twenty-five,

---

21   New York Estates, Powers and Trusts Law §1-2.9(a).

or even older. You're not locked into distribution right at the legal age of majority. The trust establishes the manner of distribution of money and assets to the child, and this is a key feature of such trusts and is known as "controlled distribution of assets." When establishing the trust, the grantors can state how and when beneficiaries receive their inheritance. This approach provides flexibility and helps ensure responsible management of assets.

The trust puts a buffer in place between the underaged child and the assets. Until then, the minor's trust is managed by a trustee, who is an adult responsible for overseeing and managing the assets on behalf of the minor beneficiary. The trustee essentially serves as the financial parent.

Let's say you're a parent, and both you and your spouse pass away, leaving a twelve-year-old child behind. Just as if you were alive and you were the buffer, the trustee becomes the "surrogate parent" between the minor and the money.

The twelve-year-old might stomp his foot and insist, "I want to go to Disneyland this week and next week and the week after that!" The living parent is the buffer saying, "No, we're going to Disneyland only once because we control the money, and we know what's good for you."

The trustee makes the same judgment calls so that the minor child doesn't use up that money. Now, buying a car so the older minor can drive to school is a good use of the money. But buying a Bugatti is where the trustee acts as a buffer to say, "Sorry, not happening." The trustee decides that a used but serviceable KIA would suffice.

The trustee of a minor's trust thus acts as a surrogate parent, protecting and managing the child's money.

Guardians

If you don't have an estate plan that names the guardian of the person (the one who has physical custody of the child), and the guardian of the property (the one who controls the money), then someone has to do it. No decision is a decision, and it's usually the worst one. If you don't name the guardians, then New York State will put someone in charge of your children and their inheritance.

I'm a firm believer that you, and not some judge, should be the one choosing who gets physical custody of your child and who manages your child's inheritance on their behalf.

Remember my hopefully scary comments earlier in this book about dying intestate with minor children? Not naming the guardians has other detrimental ripples. It can cause intrafamilial conflict even if everyone is well-meaning and looking to care for your children.

You might have the wife's side of the family stepping up to do the right thing, but you might have someone on the husband's side of the family who is also well intentioned and wants to do the right thing. All good intentions aside, now the families are in competition against each other. Tragically, it can lead to once-friendly relatives throwing mud at each other to prove they are the better guardian and the others are not. Furthermore, the judge can ultimately decide that it's in the best interest of the child to appoint a public guardian and not a family member.

Excuses for Procrastination

- Reluctance to confront mortality: Many individuals find it emotionally challenging to prepare for the eventuality of their own death, as it requires confronting their mortality and the potential absence from their children's lives. This emotional difficulty often leads to procrastination in making such critical decisions.

- Difficulty in choosing a suitable guardian: Parents may struggle to identify an individual or couple who they believe can adequately fulfill the parental role and provide the care, values, and stability they desire for their minor children. The concern over making the right choice can delay the appointment of a guardian.

- Penchant for family conflict: The potential for family disagreements or conflicts regarding the appointment of a guardian can be a deterrent. Parents may worry about causing discord among relatives or facing opposition from family members who may have differing opinions about who should be appointed as the guardian.

Whatever your reasons to avoid deciding on guardianship, without an estate plan, the Surrogate's Court will appoint a trustee to manage the minor's assets and a guardian to have physical custody of the minor. This can cause long, drawn-out proceedings and often intense family conflict. Ultimately, it will be the court, and not the deceased, that will appoint trustees and guardians for the children. Although it is most common for the court to appoint family members as trustees and guardians, this is not guaranteed to occur. Moreover, if any portion of your assets are needed to pay for your child's more pressing needs, such as education, clothing, or living costs, prior approval of the court will be necessary, and that takes time.

On top of the time factor, there may be additional costs and fees. The court may require the posting of a bond, which leads to annual premiums. Courts will require an annual accounting of income and expenses, which will add extra expenses. Furthermore, the ability of trustees to invest the trust's holdings may be limited.

Another issue with the court appointing a guardian is that the court becomes a quasi-co-guardian to whomever they appoint. That means that every time that trustee wants to make an expenditure, they have to ask the court for permission. Want to go to Disneyland this year? Petition the court. Need to buy a car for the minor? Petition the court. Also, you have annual accountings you have to file, and that runs up time and expenses.

You want to make these decisions for your children. You don't want a court to decide and potentially bypass family or appoint family that you would not choose.

Whether you name someone or the court does, the court will always make a decision in the best interest of the child, true. But there is an easier way, and it is to make and document these decisions yourself and do it now. By putting that person's name in a will or minor's trust, you get amazing deference from the court. So unless the person is legally not qualified, the court is generally going to side with you and appoint that person.

By naming the trustee and guardian, there is no third party involved in every decision about financial expenditure, and you're avoiding additional fees and delays.

The Right Guardian

I advise clients to avoid picking married couples as trustees/guardians, because couples get divorced. You should also not pick someone to handle the trust that isn't experienced in managing money. Don't pick the guardian or the minor's trustee because "they deserve it," or "we've always liked her," or "she's the big sister."

I've had clients from large families pick a close friend to be the trustee and guardian of their children. Pick a person to raise your kids as if you're still around, watching. The goal is to name a competent person whom you trust and respect to do the right thing.

As I stated earlier, you can set the age of majority in your trust document—anything at or over your state's legal age of majority. Unless circumstances warrant it, I try to dissuade people from making the trust span the beneficiary's lifetime. A forty-year-old adult should be experienced enough to handle the inheritance. Also, if you have a twelve-year-old and pick your thirty-year-old brother to be the trustee, and you've created a lifetime trust, most likely the thirty-year-old brother isn't going to be around for the beneficiary's whole lifetime. Who takes over as trustee? You now may have a judge deciding who the successor trustee will be to your now sixty-two-year-old "child."

If you don't create a trust and the court creates the minor's trust for you, as soon as the child reaches that state's age of majority (eighteen in most states), they get all the money and assets in a lump sum. Now we're back to square one.

This is the same for beneficiaries who are incompetent: You want to make a trust so they have access to enough money to help them in life. You can still help that person who isn't able to make their own financial decisions to inherit the money through a controlled distribution mechanism and get the use of it as opposed to not giving it to them at all.

CHAPTER 16

The Watchdog of Wealth—
A Trust Protector Guards Your Legacy

*You can never protect yourself 100 percent.
What you do is protect yourself as much as
possible and mitigate risk to an acceptable
degree. You can never remove all risk.*
—Kevin Mitnick

I often have to clarify to my clients that a "trust protector" is a human being and not a document or a mechanism. The trust protector is a fiduciary—a third party. In other words, it is an individual who is not the trustee.

You most commonly see trust protectors in irrevocable trusts. As previously discussed, irrevocable trusts are difficult or impossible to amend, change, or update. We all acknowledge, however, that what was good five years ago may not be good today. Rules and regulations change, and people change. There are marriages, divorces, deaths, and births. That means we need some way of allowing flexibility in an inflexible world.

What you do is include trust protector provisions into the trust document upon its creation. These provisions allow a degree of flexibility in an otherwise inflexible, irrevocable trust. A trust protector (not the trustee) can make certain changes and updates to the irrevocable trust. You make it as broad or as restrictive as needed. I advise clients to make the provisions as broad as possible, because the broader the powers, the more flexibility they provide.

The number one thing a trust protector is able to do is modify trust provisions. Remember that you're making amendments to an irrevocable trust, which is by all the usual definitions non-amendable. If there is a law change—such as recently happened when the IRS codified that an irrevocable trust doesn't get step-up in basis unless there is particular language in a trust—what to do? A trust protector can update the trust to ensure the trust permits the basis increase. If you don't have a trust protector provision, you would not have had a way to make amendments to the trust allowing it to change with the tax law.

Having a trust protector with the ability to modify, change, add, or remove provisions based on tax law, trust law, and estate law is highly advantageous for turning a static document into more of a living, breathing document.

Frankly, I add a trust protector provision into every irrevocable trust and revocable trust I create for clients. It's insurance, really. Imagine if the trustee isn't doing the right thing. The trust protector can step in and remove that negligent trustee. In case of life changes for beneficiaries, the trust protector can modify the trust to include the new grandchild or add special needs provisions as needed. If a beneficiary should become estranged, the trust protector can remove that beneficiary. If you put something in your trust and the terms aren't clear, the trust protector can interpret those terms.

The trust protector, as an independent person, can make a distribution without having to worry about self-dealing conflicts. They can help the trustee who isn't skilled in finance, money management, or investing. Your trust protector can manage trust-owned businesses if the trustee doesn't have the experience or desire to do so. Having a trust protector does give a lot of benefits, not the least of which is insurance that your trust provisions are protected.

CHAPTER 17

Trust Checkmate: Grantor vs. Non-Grantor Trusts

These young guys are playing checkers.
I am out there playing chess.
—Kobe Bryant

I need to speak about another aspect of taxation and address how much money you might be leaving on the table when you have trusts. To determine this, we need to look at the differences between "grantor" and "non-grantor" trusts as far as how they are taxed.

Let me specify for you that with a grantor trust, the grantor is the person who creates and funds the trust and also retains certain powers or control over the trust. For a non-grantor trust, the grantor relinquishes all control and beneficial interest over the trust assets.

As alluded to in the prior chapter, in 2023, the IRS issued Revenue Rule 2003–2 determining that irrevocable trusts don't enjoy step-up in basis upon death of the grantor unless the trust property is part of the grantor's taxable estate.

Step-Up in Basis

First, let's remember what "step-up in basis" means: It is an adjustment of the cost basis of an inherited asset to its fair market value on the date of the previous owner's death—your death if you're the one who created the trust. The difference between the basis and sale determines the capital gains tax imposed.

In other words, for your heir, the cost basis of that asset is modified to equal its market value at the time of your death. So if the property is sold immediately after death, the fair market value is the date of death value and therefore there will be no capital gains tax.

Grantor Versus Non-Grantor Trusts

Grantor Trusts:

- Taxable to you during your life
- Included in your taxable estate when you pass
- Enjoy a step-up in basis upon your death

Non-Grantor Trusts:

- Pays its own taxes during your life
- Not included in your taxable estate when you pass
- Do not enjoy a step-up in basis upon your death

Attorneys who aren't experienced in estate taxation don't consider or even know how to work out whether you're better off tax-wise with a grantor trust or a non-grantor trust. Are you better off getting that step-up in basis or not? A tremendous number of nuances are involved. This is definitely a topic for analysis between you and an experienced elder law plus tax law attorney, and luckily, I'm both.

The Grantor Trust

Trust assets are taxed to the person who created the trust—the grantor—during their lifetime. When the grantor passes, the trust assets get a step-up in basis if the assets are part of the grantor's estate, potentially lowering capital gains tax for heirs.

With the grantor trust, the income tax is due by the grantor during the grantor's life. It's part of the grantor's taxable estate at death. You get the adjusted basis on the date of death.

In a grantor trust, the grantor retains certain powers or interests over the trust assets, as I stated earlier, and this retained control is a key characteristic of grantor trusts.

Grantor Trusts Provisions

- The power to revoke or amend the trust
- The ability to direct investments
- The ability to retain income interest
- The power to change trust beneficiaries
- The ability to substitute assets or borrow from the trust without adequate security

The Non-Grantor Trust

With the non-grantor trust, the grantor is relinquishing all control and benefits. Once established, a non-grantor trust operates as a separate legal entity, independent of the grantor. The trust pays its own income taxes, and assets are not included in the grantor's taxable estate at death, avoiding estate tax but missing the step-up in basis benefit.

Non-Grantor Trusts Provisions

- No power to revoke: The grantor can't undo the trust or take back the assets.
  - No power to change beneficiaries: The grantor can't add or remove beneficiaries from the trust.
- No power to distribute income to themselves: The grantor can't direct income from the trust to be paid to them.
- Separate tax entity: A non-grantor trust files its own tax return and is taxed on its income separately from the grantor.

Simply put, here is what that IRS rule means as regards the step-up in basis (or not):

- If you, the grantor, are going to be paying estate taxes, you're paying income taxes on the asset you put in the trust, you get a step-up in basis.

- If the irrevocable trust is paying its own taxes and not the grantor, it does not get a step-up in basis.

When planning, we want to make sure that we analyze whether or not you're better off having a grantor trust or a non-grantor trust.

Ninety percent of the clients that are beneath the estate tax exclusion threshold won't have to worry about paying an estate tax. Of the clients who come into my office with $10 million or less in assets, 90 percent of them are going to want to establish grantor trusts to preserve the step-up in basis. Larger estates, however, may benefit from a non-grantor trust, especially if they exceed the estate tax exclusion threshold and could be subject to estate tax.

There are inheritance tax and capital gains tax trade-offs. We need to discuss and calculate whether capital gains taxes on appreciated assets outweigh potential estate taxes. For instance, paying a long-term capital gains tax of 30–35 percent could be preferable to the higher 45 percent inheritance tax rate. Trusts often have higher income tax rates, so comparing personal and trust tax rates is an analysis we must do. You don't get this level of planning from a shelf or an attorney who only practices real estate closings.

The Mechanics

The general distinctions between grantor trusts and non-grantor trusts:

- A trust is considered a grantor trust if the grantor (the person who creates and funds the trust) retains certain powers or benefits over the trust assets, and the trust's income is taxed to the grantor on their personal tax return.

- A trust is generally considered a non-grantor trust when the grantor relinquishes all control and benefits over the trust assets, and the trust is treated as a separate legal and tax entity.

You might wonder how to change from one to the other status. That takes us back to the benefits of having a trust protector. In irrevocable trusts, a trust protector can adjust the trust's status (grantor or non-grantor) based on changing tax laws and the grantor's needs. The trust protector can add provisions to a non-grantor trust, such as a "life estate" clause that grants an individual (known as the life tenant) the right to use and occupy a property for the duration of their lifetime.

Your Best Interest

You have to compare taxes on your income versus taxes on the trust. Deciding whether to establish the grantor versus non-grantor trust calls for having an experienced attorney ask you the right questions and make the calculations.

Because trusts typically have a higher income tax rate, we have to weigh a number of factors:

- The amount of capital gains that may be assessed
- The inheritance tax thresholds and rates
- The trust income tax rate
- Your personal income tax rate

If you went to an attorney who does corporate lit-igation to do your trust, they may not even know about these nuances. Come to me and discuss your goals and needs—every situation I look at goes through the lens of tax mitigation, the lens of asset and wealth protection, the lens of protecting your legacy. Working with an experienced elder law tax attorney to handle the non-grantor or grantor trust decision protects you from IRS and Medicaid scrutiny.

Uncle Sam wants your money. Medicaid wants your money. New York State wants your money. You want your heirs and beneficiaries to have your money. A template will from the internet can't analyze these factors, and an attorney who is not experienced in estate planning and taxation will not address all your goals or be aware of all the available options.

CHAPTER 18

Protect Your Castle—A Moat May Not Be Enough

Government can't deliver a free lunch to the country as a whole. It can, however, determine who pays for lunch.
—Warren Buffett

I have clients who are what I like to characterize as house rich and cash poor. Their primary asset is their home, which is usually 100 percent paid off. Their only concern is that they worked hard for the home they live in, and they want to make sure that their property passes to their children and isn't taken away by the government. While they want to see that their children get the house, they also want to make sure they have a place to live until their passing.

It seems everyone has heard horror stories about transferring the house to the child, and the child (or the child's spouse) turns around and kicks out the parent. My clients are looking for a strategy on how to pass this property to their child in the future while securing their own living conditions in the present.

The strategies I will present here are what I call "protecting your castle." Each strategy applies to land and buildings only, with a primary focus on asset protection. Capital gains strategies and long-term care planning are wrapped up in each strategy as well.

This merits a reminder: You buy a house for $100,000 (cost basis). You sell that house for $1 million. You then add $250,000 exemption for single owner and $150,000 in improvements. According to Uncle Sam, you made $500,000 in profit. If you sold the property, you would be looking at somewhere around $175,000 in capital gains tax. If you pass that same house to your children via inheritance, if the children sell the day after you pass, there will be no capital gains tax. This is because your tax basis is adjusted to the fair market value (step-up in basis) as of the date of your passing.

We want to employ a strategy that sets out to accomplish most, if not all, of the following goals:

- Protect your house

- Preserve your right to stay in your house, worry-free, for the rest of your life

- Mitigate the profit to reduce capital gains taxes

- Get long-term care Medicaid asset protection

Life Estate

One simple planning strategy is to create a "life estate" in your home. A life estate isn't a trust. It is, instead, a re-organizing of the ownership of your house to accomplish your protection goals.

Life estate planning in real property, simply described, has you transfer title or ownership of your house to your children. But—and this is the important piece—the transfer isn't complete because your children's ownership in the house is restricted so that you retain the right to reside in the house until you pass away. Once you pass away, the transfer of ownership is complete.

You, or the person who retains the life interest, is called the "life tenant." Your children, or whomever you chose to name on the title, are called the "remaindermen." The government considers this arrangement as an incomplete gift to the title owners. A life estate in real property is typically established by transferring the property in a zero consideration, or no-money, exchange.

The same documents you need in a home purchase are the documents you need to do a life estate. It is essentially the same deed, except the deed has additional language saying that you, the grantor or the seller/transferor, retains a life estate. This language places a restriction on the title owner's rights to do whatever they want with the property.

What are the benefits of a life estate? A life estate avoids probate because you've already made the transfer. If you put your children as the title owner in a life estate, the children become the 100 percent title owner upon your death without passing through probate. The ownership immediately transfers at the life tenant's death.

Transferring a piece of property into a life estate is a low-cost strategy, and the property, with some restrictions, becomes exempt from Medicaid's consideration when the applicable look-back period expires. Furthermore, the property becomes and remains exempt from Medicaid as long as the property isn't sold during the life tenant's lifetime.

Note

If you have a **life estate** and decide to sell the property while you're still alive, you are converting a Medicaid-exempt asset into a **Medicaid-countable asset**. This means that the money from the sale will now be counted as part of your assets, which could put you over Medicaid's asset limit and affect your eligibility.

On the other hand, if your property is in a **Medicaid Asset Protection Trust (MAPT)**, your trustee can sell the property, keep the money safely inside the trust, and even buy another property with it—all without affecting your Medicaid eligibility. The assets in the trust remain protected and do not count against Medicaid's asset limits.

You keep your property tax exemptions and credits. You get the benefit of a step-up in basis upon the life tenant's death. The cost of setting up the life estate is low, and you have Medicaid advantages.

There are more advantages, or as I see them, protections. Your children typically can't get a mortgage on the house without you signing off on it. They can't evict you, nor can they charge you rent. Any income produced by the house (renting out a room or a floor) stays with you, the life tenant.

The government sees you as the owner. You are still primarily responsible for all the obligations of home ownership. You pay the bills, taxes, repairs, upkeep. You get and pay the homeowner insurance and the property taxes.

Now, if you can't meet your financial obligations of home ownership, the title owner obviously doesn't want you to lose the house because you haven't paid your property tax. But if they pay the bills, they get the deduction, not you.

We just discussed the "big print." Now let's grab our magnifying glass for the "fine print." Just as your children can't sell or mortgage the house without your permission, the same goes for you. You can't sell or get a mortgage without the remaindermen signing off. While a life estate is considered an incomplete gift, the property is nevertheless an asset of the remaindermen.

If your children aren't good with money, and they have creditors, now those creditors have another asset to go after. If they file for bankruptcy, your home is the remaindermen's asset and exposed in bankruptcy. If your children are going through those college financial aid applications for their children (your grandchildren), they have to list this as an asset.

It is an asset of the remaindermen. If you had to sell—and you as life tenant and your children as third-party owners agree to it—you may be giving your children a capital gains tax if they are not also residing in the home. If the property is sold during the life tenant's lifetime, there is no basis step-up. The basis step-up only occurs if the sale happens after the life tenant passes away.

In every interview I conduct with a client where we may want to explore the life estate strategy, I always ask them, "Do you plan on dying in this house? Is this your forever home?" If the answer is no, then, from a Medicaid perspective, the life estate option is a bad plan. If there's a chance that you'll be selling your home before you pass, the Medicaid Asset Protection Trust (MAPT) is the better option. A MAPT allows you to sell the house you own in New York and purchase a house in Utah (all done within the trust as previously explained) with no effect on your Medicaid eligibility. There is no look-back reset, and you have greater flexibility and mobility.

With the life estate transfer, you're changing a house into cash. You essentially changed an exempt asset into a non-exempt asset. A life estate plan is a good idea only if you plan this property to be a forever house. You can't sell that house and retain the exemption.

Let's look at what happens—and has to happen—when selling a life estate property during your (life tenant) lifetime.

First of all, the house can't be sold unless both the remaindermen and the life tenant sign off on it. Next, technically speaking, if you have two children, and you're a life tenant, and you all decide that you're going to sell the property, we evaluate what the life tenant's life expectancy might be. We use an IRS actuarial table that says you, the 85-year-old life tenant, are expected to live another five years.

If your property is worth $1 million, then the value of that life tenant equals $100,000. So technically, if you sold your million-dollar house, you're only going to get $100,000, and the remaindermen split the difference. If your life tenant is equal to $200,000, technically you get the $200,000 and each of your two children would collect

$400,000. They could decide that they don't want it, but now they've made a gift to you.

This is important especially if the remaindermen are estranged, because you now risk the good child/bad child scenario. Everyone might have been a good child when you made the transfer, but life can throw you curveballs.

I have a client who had two children and established a life estate for the parent where the children were the remaindermen. When the life estate was established, everyone was happily getting along, and the goal was to protect the house. Several years later, unfortunately, the "bad" child became estranged from the family because of certain life choices. The "good" child remained with the parent as their caregiver. The good child and parent decided they had to sell the house. They had to first find the estranged child and ask them permission to sell the house. The estranged child said no and demanded more money in exchange for their agreement to sell. My client ended up suing, in what we call a "petition action," to force them to sell the house. Time and money was wasted because of the need to litigate.

Keep in mind that this type of unfortunate family and legal drama happens if the remaindermen become estranged or if they pass away before the life tenant passes away—or turn to a life of crime.

As time passes, you have to accept that you might have other people involved in the life estate—perhaps your child's spouse or your grandchildren. I've seen a case where the life tenant's son got married afterward and gained a stepson.

The son was the remainderman. When the son passed away, ownership passed to the surviving daughter-in-law who then also passed away—all while Mom was still alive as the life tenant of the property. Now the Mom has someone who is on title as a partner that she really doesn't know.

Every conversation I've had with clients about this says, "Oh, my children are great." Maybe yes, maybe no. I don't know your family.

I also remind them that whether their kids are great people or not, life happens, death happens, and change is the only constant. There is a risk someone you don't know or trust ends up owning your house.

> **Blood may be thicker than water, but money is thicker than blood.**
> —Boss Hogg,
> *Dukes of Hazzard*

This discussion with my clients can potentially make a life estate sound like a horrible deal for almost anybody. But it's a great deal. I repeat, it's great for Medicaid asset protection at a lower cost than a MAPT. It's great for capital gains mitigation.

You should consider a life estate only because it is great for you and your circumstances. All these plans, strategies, and wealth protection measures that we've gone through are not cookie-cutter. Each of my clients has different circumstances, goals, and ideas about how to organize what they possess and how their heirs and beneficiaries should access their legacy.

You have to ask what the cost-benefit analysis shows you. What are the pros and what are the cons? If it doesn't fit, then don't use it. But you need to get someone who knows what they're doing, who can educate you on the pros and cons for you to make a decision.

Now, remember what I said in the beginning. My goal and my role as an attorney, my philosophy, is not to tell you what you must do. I want to understand your goals and present options for what you could do. I try to give you more than one path to accomplish your goals, and then you choose.

The Transfer on Death Deed

Another aspect of real property management is the "Transfer on Death Deed" (TODD) that recently became legal in New York (July 2024). It exists in other states. Every state has its own rules.

If you choose to make a TODD, the property immediately passes to the beneficiaries as soon as you pass away. There is no probate, but there are conditions.

Say you're the grantor naming your three adult children as beneficiaries. Ownership by the beneficiaries can't be made in unequal shares. That is one condition. When you pass away with a TODD, it says each of the three gets a one-third share.

If one beneficiary child passes away and leaves behind his own children, the one-third share doesn't go to those grandchildren. It isn't inheritable by the beneficiary's heirs.

It will go to the other two people listed on the deed, again in equal shares, but not filter down to the deceased beneficiary's heirs.

Another condition of the TODD is that the beneficiary takes the property subject to all its liens and encumbrances. If you have a mortgage, the mortgage is based on you. It isn't based on your child's situation. Thus, if you do a TODD, the child still isn't part of the mortgage. When you pass away and the beneficiary takes over, the mortgage company can't say they don't like you as a mortgagee and accelerate the note. The lender can't accelerate the loan or force a refinancing. The beneficiary must continue to make the payments as the original grantor was. If there are any other loans or liens, beneficiaries take them on.

If the grantor is a joint tenant with right of survivorship, the other joint tenant will take 100 percent title upon the grantor's death, not the beneficiary(ies). This ends the TODD, and thus your beneficiaries get knocked out of any interest in the property. If the grantor owns in common, the grantor's interest will pass to the beneficiary(ies) upon the grantor's death.

We want to make sure the property is owned in common and not in joint tenancy.

There are other potential downsides. The TODD doesn't give protection from creditors. If the grantor's estate can't satisfy a claim, or if there is a right of election from a spouse, the claim can be enforceable against a TODD property. They have to make the claim within eighteen months of death. That could mean that if this is part of your estate, and you have $1 million of estate tax, that tax will have to be paid off this deed.

Another downside is that there is no Medicaid protection on the TODD because it is your property, your countable asset, and Medicaid will have a lien on it. It doesn't give you the asset protection that a MAPT or life estate would provide you.

The upsides are that you retain ownership and complete control of the property throughout your lifetime (contrary to the life estate process discussed above). If you leave the property to heirs, they won't go through a probate proceeding.

An experienced attorney like me will know the upsides but also the downsides to any choice available to you and present them up-front so you can decide from facts. No single guidebook (even this one) can do that for you.

CHAPTER 19

Looking into the Crystal Ball— What May Be Coming

I am not in the business of reading tea leaves.
I don't have a crystal ball.
—Christine Lagarde

This book, which I primarily drafted in the last part of 2024, provides an overview of the current estate and inheritance tax laws applicable under both federal and New York State jurisdictions. I aimed to offer a comprehensive understanding of the legal framework governing estate and inheritance taxes and to highlight key provisions, exemptions, and rates as established by the relevant statutes and regulations.

This overview has always only been intended to inform and guide you regarding the implications of these laws on estate planning and inheritance matters so that you may have informed discussions of your needs and options with a qualified attorney.

Potential Changes Under the 2025 Trump Administration

We have now, as of January 2025, a new federal ball game called a "change of presidency," with the accompanying shuffle in the composition of the US Congress. The incoming candidates have already given us a preview of some of their proposed new legislation (if you've read the media, at any rate).

My purpose in this last chapter is to share with you some of those potential changes to estate and inheritance tax laws under the new administration since it is (as I write) still too early for Congress to have acted on most of them. *Potential* is the keyword here. My analysis is based on the current understanding of policy proposals and public statements made by the incoming Trump administration and other lawmakers. As these proposals are subject to legislative process and potential modifications (or outright rejection), the information provided should be considered preliminary and subject to change. Naturally, some, all, or none of these policies may be implemented. Please do not take anything here as an endorsement or rejection of any policy or party; it's just a discussion of what is being considered by lawmakers.

Given federal and New York State jurisdictions, any changes to estate and inheritance tax laws may have significant implications for your estate planning strategies. We estate tax planners are closely monitoring these ongoing developments.

Also important to note is that this analysis focuses exclusively on estate and inheritance tax implications and does not encompass considerations related to income tax.

All that disclaimer language is to say that you will need to be sure to consult an estate attorney (or a certain Master of Laws in Taxation perhaps) when making your estate plan.

Some Potential Estate Tax Policy Proposals We Are Monitoring

Note that a number of tax policies I will discuss below will be new to you as I haven't presented them in earlier pages. There are so many strategies to keep up with that, again, I must encourage you to consult a tax professional who likewise understands estate planning and estate taxation.

Repeal of the Estate Tax

One of the most significant changes discussed with the election of Donald Trump is talk abOut the complete repeal of the federal estate tax. This would eliminate the federal inheritance tax, no matter the value of the estate. Given the current legislative landscape and the historical challenges in garnering sufficient support for the repeal of estate taxes at death, the future status of such a complete elimination of inheritance taxes remains uncertain. It is possible, however, that with shifting political dynamics and increasing advocacy from certain interest groups, there could be renewed efforts aimed at altering these taxes.

A potential scenario might involve a bipartisan legislative proposal that seeks to phase out estate taxes over a decade, gradually reducing the tax rate until it is repealed, as we saw with the 2001 and 2003 Bush tax cuts. This could gain traction if it includes provisions that address concerns related to revenue loss, such as introducing alternative taxation mechanisms or tightening existing tax loopholes.

Reduction of the Gift Tax Rates

Alongside changes to the estate tax, discussions and legislative proposals surrounding the reduction of gift tax rates and adjustments to the annual exclusion exemption at death continue to be a focal point of debate among policymakers.

An example of this ongoing debate is a proposal introduced in Congress, which aims to lower the gift tax rate from 40 percent to 35 percent and increase the annual exclusion exemption from $15,000 to $20,000 per recipient. This proposed adjustment reflects the growing concern among individuals and financial advisors about optimizing wealth transfer strategies under the current tax regime. No definitive changes have been enacted yet; however, the potential for modification remains a pertinent issue for individuals and advisors in wealth management and estate planning fields.

Changes to Step-Up in Basis

The incoming administration considered altering the rules around the step-up in basis at death. This could have an impact on how capital gains are calculated on inherited assets, potentially leading to higher taxes on the sale of such assets. Conversely, there have been some talks in Congress about eliminating or curtailing the step-up in basis for inherited assets.

Currently, assets inherited are subject to a step-up in basis to their current market value, minimizing capital gains taxes if sold. Proposed changes include eliminating this step-up, and potentially increasing tax burdens on inherited assets.

Introduction of Unrealized Capital Gains Tax at Death

The imposition of taxes on unrealized capital gains at death remains a topic of significant debate and legislative interest in the United States since at least 2023. Currently, unrealized capital gains are not taxed at the time of death. Instead, the tax basis of an inherited asset is stepped up to its market value at the time of the decedent's death.

This step-up in basis means that the capital gains accumulated during the decedent's lifetime are never taxed if the assets aren't sold before death. Legislative proposals have been introduced in the past to change this system and impose taxes on unrealized capital gains upon death, aiming to close what is seen as a significant loophole in the tax code that benefits wealthy estates. These proposals have not been enacted into law.

The debate around this issue is ongoing, with arguments focusing on the potential revenue to be gained by taxing these unrealized gains against the challenges of implementing such a tax, including valuing complex assets and the impact on family-owned businesses and farms.

Elimination of Generation-Skipping Transfer Tax

We have seen a recurring debate among policymakers about eliminating the generation-skipping transfer tax (GSTT), which applies to transfers to beneficiaries two or more generations below the donor, thus simplifying estate planning for multigenerational wealth transfer.

Despite various proposals introduced over the years aiming to repeal or modify the GSTT to alleviate the tax burden on transfers to subsequent generations, no significant legislative action has been taken to eliminate the tax. The GSTT, designed to tax transfers of property that skip a generation, continues to play a critical role in our estate and gift tax regime. It imposes a tax on both outright gifts and transfers in trust to or for the benefit of individuals more than one generation below the donor, effectively preventing the avoidance of estate and gift taxes through the use of generation-skipping transfers.

Adjustments to Valuation Discounts

The administration reviewed "valuation discounts" for estate tax purposes, particularly those applied to family-owned businesses and real estate. Tightening these rules could increase the taxable value of an estate.

Valuation discounts are a critical tool in estate planning. These discounts allow for the reduction of the estate's value through various mechanisms, including minority discounts or lack of marketability discounts when transferring closely held business interests or other illiquid assets. These discounts are applied to lower the taxable value of an estate, thereby potentially reducing the estate tax burden.

Despite ongoing discussions and debates within the legal and financial communities about the appropriateness and future of valuation discounts, the current legal framework remains unchanged.

My Recommendations

In consideration of the evolving landscape of federal and New York State tax laws, it is imperative to adopt a proactive approach to your estate planning. The following recommendations are designed to optimize your estate's tax positioning in anticipation of potential legislative changes:

- Review and update your estate plan regularly to ensure it aligns with current tax laws and your personal circumstances.

- Consider establishing trusts that can offer flexibility and tax advantages, such as revocable trusts for estate management and irrevocable trusts for asset protection and tax savings.

- Utilize the annual gift tax exclusions to gradually transfer wealth to beneficiaries, thereby reducing the taxable estate.

- Explore opportunities for charitable giving, which can provide tax benefits while supporting causes important to you.

- Engage with a tax professional or estate planning attorney who is well versed in both federal and New York State tax laws to tailor a strategy that best suits your unique situation.

Implementing these strategies requires careful consideration and professional guidance to ensure compliance with current laws and to effectively manage potential future changes.

While I have provided a basic overview of estate and inheritance tax planning considerations in light of potential changes under the new 2025 Trump administration, individuals and families must stay informed of these developments, as they could significantly impact estate planning strategies and tax liabilities.

Given the complexities of federal and New York State tax laws, you should consult with a tax professional to navigate these changes effectively. Proactive planning and ongoing review of estate plans will be essential to optimize tax outcomes and ensure that estate planning objectives are met.

As my practice area includes estate and tax planning, I closely monitor legislative updates and, accordingly, adjust my estate planning strategies for my clients as changes occur. If you don't have an estate planning and tax attorney at this time, contact me, and we can discuss your needs and concerns.

CONCLUSION

The future is unknown, and none of us can foresee the changes to our personal life or political policies. A person's health or financial situation tomorrow can't be known. A person can become disabled, injured, or pass away at any time. Anyone can strike it rich or require public assistance at any time in any number of ways, some gradual, some sudden.

An estate plan is a legal written document whose basic purpose is to specify how your property and possessions are to be distributed after your death. Your estate plan should direct who gets your property, and proper planning can avoid estate taxes for you and your heirs as well as plan for the specific and special needs of your beneficiaries.

Some people (but not you, of course) may have read every page of this book yet still think that they don't have enough money or own valuable enough property to warrant getting an estate plan, or that they're too young to need one.

Believing you're too young, not rich enough, or too healthy now to worry about something as confusing and uncomfortable as an estate plan is just wrong thinking.

The best time to put a comprehensive plan in place was yesterday.

The second-best time is now.

Procrastination and fear of making an estate plan can cause delays that may create a situation where it becomes too late for you to make a plan.

Are any of the following circumstances true for you?

- You own a house or condo, even mortgaged to the hilt right now
- You don't own a thing but have lots of saved cash
- You have minor children
- You have adult dependents
- You are concerned about your future health care costs
- You worry about navigating Medicare and Medicaid
- You don't like certain family members
- You hate paying taxes
- You play the lotto
- You are currently breathing

Just one of them being true is reason enough to start working with me to create an estate plan.

Tax codes and regulations constantly change. Personal financial upturns and downturns occur. We move from one state or country to another. There are births, deaths, marriages, and divorces. Our personal goals change. The people around us ten years ago have disappeared from our lives, and others have entered it.

Life is constantly evolving. These constantly changing situations are what make not only drafting but updating your estate plan necessary. Estate plans can be changed and adjusted at any time to adapt to these changes. The laws of intestate, however, don't change with your personal situation.

Invest in yourself. Invest in your legacy. You can disinherit Uncle Sam by investing time and effort in drafting an estate plan. Speak with an experienced attorney about your concerns, your wishes, and your goals. There are solutions for you. Don't trust cookie-cutter solutions, but seek solutions that are tailored to your needs, wishes, and circumstances.

My goal with this book wasn't just to talk about planning strategies but also to light a fire under your butt to start planning (do you feel the heat yet?). It was also to calm you by presenting potential solutions—some strategies you may not have known about. Ultimately, you have to go to someone who knows what they're doing in taxation, in elder planning, in estate planning.

I help clients every day to plan so that they experience the most comfortable retirement years possible. My concern is to help you keep as much of your money during your lifetime as possible, while also helping your heirs keep as much as possible through proper tax and estate planning.

Planning means that you disinherit the taxman to the greatest degree allowable. Tax efficiency isn't for the weak of heart, but with expert guidance and planning in advance of your needs, it can be achieved. You must also set things up in a written, legally binding plan so you decide who gets your assets and how. You love your heirs and are passionate about your charitable giving. Make things as tax-efficient as possible for your survivors too. Avoid the emotional roller coaster of probate (and its costs) for them. We can do that with proper planning.

Planning also means avoiding the stress of future costs of your long-term health care needs. You've paid into that system your whole life. Proper planning will ensure that you get the care you need and want on Uncle's dime.

If you already have an estate plan, I recommend that you have it reviewed at any major life event (marriage, death, lotto win, birth of a child or grandchild, move to another state), but at least once every three to five years. If your tax advisor or attorney calls or emails to say, "A new change is coming in the tax code," you need to revisit your plan at that time as well.

Writing the plan is first. Revisiting your plan is keeping it relevant.

Your time is the most valuable commodity you have. Thank you for spending it with me. I look forward to meeting you and having our next conversation.

ASK YOURSELF

If you're still on the fence regarding discussing and drafting an estate plan, ask yourself these questions:

1. Do you have dependents, either minor children, elder parents, or other individuals? What would become of them if you passed away today, with the plan you currently have in place (or because you have no plan)?

2. If you should unexpectedly pass away, do you have a plan as to who will take care of your children, or are you comfortable with a court deciding what's in the best interest of your kids?

3. If a tragedy happens to you tomorrow, do you have a plan to care for your child or family member who has special needs?

4. Do you know how much of your assets could be exposed to taxes, legal fees, and delays when you pass away?

5. Are you okay with New York State deciding what happens to your legacy when you pass away, or would you rather be the one dictating what happens to your legacy?

6. What is your backup plan if an accident or sudden illness leaves you unable to make decisions about your health and finances?

7. Are you concerned about an undeserving family member taking or receiving your inheritance or contesting your last wishes?

8. Do you have a plan in place to avoid the financial chaos your family might face if you were to pass away suddenly without a solid estate plan?

9. Are you concerned about the possibility of you or your parents losing their life savings or home to long-term care costs without a Medicaid plan?

10. If an unexpected health event occurred, how quickly would your or your parents' assets be at risk of being used up without a Medicaid plan? How comfortable are you with that level of risk?

ASK ME

So you decided to consult a tax and estate planning lawyer. Use this "cheat sheet" of frequently asked questions and their answers to prepare for our first consultation:

1. What information do I need to bring to the consultation?

    a. All your personal information and the addresses and phone numbers of your heirs and others on your family tree

    b. All your financial information, such as bank accounts, IRAs, life insurance, real estate, stocks, bonds, and investments

2. What is the difference between a will and a trust?

    a. A will is a legal document where you set out your wishes on how your personal and real property is to be distributed after you pass. After you pass, you have to submit the will to the Surrogate's Court and go through a probate process that could last twelve months or more.

    b. A will does not provide Medicaid asset protection.

    c. A revocable trust is a legal document similar to a will, except the personal and real property in the trust does not have to go through Surrogate's Court before they are distributed. You can change any trust term or even revoke it entirely.

d. A revokable trust does not provide Medicaid asset protection.

e. An irrevocable trust is a legal document that is similar to a revocable trust, except, generally, once it is created it can't be changed, amended, or revoked unless special circumstances exist. Typically used in Medicaid asset protection and advanced estate tax planning.

3. What happens if I pass away without a will?

a. Your personal and real property will be distributed according to what the government statute dictates, and not how you may want to have your property distributed. There is no estate taxation planning, no Medicaid asset protection planning, no vulnerable beneficiary planning, and no other type of planning, the money just goes where the government wants.

4. Is there a minimum amount of assets needed to create a will or estate plan?

e. No. Even if you have a small amount of assets, I always recommend that you have a will for these reasons:

- For random or unforeseen circumstances (A person may receive money after they pass away; for example, if someone passes after a personal injury or wrongful death action.)
- To establish guardianships over children under the age of eighteen
- To choose your executor or the trustee/ guardian for children or disabled persons
- To choose who gets your property or who does not get your property
- To specify your funeral wishes, such as your final resting place, whether you would like to be buried or cremated, or if you have any funeral service requests

5. What does my executor have to do?

   a. The executor is a person named by you and appointed by the Surrogate's Court who is responsible for collecting the probate assets, paying the estate debts, and distributing the estate assets according to the terms of the will and the law.

6. What property has to go through the probate process?

    a. Non-probate assets or accounts that pass to beneficiaries by operation of law, such as joint ownership of property or bank accounts, insurance policies that list beneficiaries, etc., don't have to go through the probate process.

    b. Probate property, assets, or accounts are owned or titled only by the deceased or don't have listed beneficiaries. This has to go through the probate process.

7. Are there other documents I should have prepared in addition to my will?

    a. Power of attorney to name someone to help you with your financial affairs

    b. Health care proxy to name someone to help you with your medical affairs

    c. Living will document that tells your health care practitioner what you want to happen if you're in a permanent vegetative state, without hope of recovery, and are only being kept alive by artificial means

8. Will I have to pay inheritance taxes when I pass away?

    a. Whether you have to pay inheritance taxes is based upon the federal and state estate tax exemption thresholds when and in which state you pass away.

    b. Thresholds change, often annually.

9. What topics should I talk to the lawyer about during our consultation?

    a. Who you want to be included or excluded in sharing your inheritance

    b. If you have gifts to specific people, whether lump-sum cash gifts, collectibles or antiques, charitable donations, wedding rings, etc.

    c. What, if any, your inheritance tax exposure is now and could be in the future

    d. Who you want to have physical custody of and financial control over your minor children and/or special needs adult children

e. Why protecting your assets from Medicaid is important and how to do so

f. What happens to your real estate holdings

10. How long is a will valid?

a. A will is valid forever, as long as it is executed correctly.

b. It is recommended to review your plan every three to five years and under the following circumstances:

c. After any inheritance tax changes

d. After a family life-changing event such as a wedding, death, birth, divorce, etc.

e. Upon any other change in intrafamily relationships such as estrangement or reconciliation

ABOUT THE AUTHOR

Stephen A. Bonfa is a native New Yorker and Brooklynite. He was a championship high school wrestler, and today he now wrestles against the tax code for his family, clients, friends, and other attorneys. He enjoys getting out for white water rafting and other activities with his wife, Carmela, and their teenage twins, Anthony and Isabella.

Stephen is a third-generation Italian-American whose grandfather was a tailor before he immigrated to the United States. His grandparents both worked in the garment industry's sweatshops while they raised their four children. His father worked in food sales. Stephen is the first professional in his family and built his law practice by helping middle-class families to preserve and pass on their inheritance. He says, "As my success was built standing on the shoulders of my parents and grandparents, I offer my shoulders to help others do the same."

Stephen and his family live in Long Island, New York. Stephen moved to Long Island to be closer to his fantastic mother- and father-in-law. He moved there from Brooklyn where, as he says, "I was living as a good Italian son in the basement of my mother's house, and now, like a good Italian son, my mother lives in an apartment in my house. I never left home."

Though he celebrates twenty-five years in the legal profession, he went to college with no plan to train as or become an attorney but had his mind set on a career teaching history. To fill a slot in his schedule, he took a class that required working in public service. That service landed him at the NYC Queens District Attorney's Office (because they were the first ones who said yes).

At the district attorney's office, he walked into the courtroom and was hit by a bolt of lightning: He knew he wanted to be a lawyer. As this occurred in his last year in college, he had to take a year off to study and take the LSATs. He got accepted to New York Law School, passed the bar examination on the first attempt (upon learning of Stephen's bar passage, his father proudly exclaimed that he "was now smarter than the Kennedys!") and has never looked back.

Having decided on a career in law, he has served in multiple government agencies, including as an Assistant District Attorney, an NYC Administrative Law Judge, an NYC Police Department Attorney, and an NYC Department of Buildings Managing Attorney.

Stephen earned a Master of Laws in Taxation. He is admitted to practice law in New York State, the United States Eastern and Southern District Courts, and the United States Tax Court.

Today, his primary areas of practice are estate planning, Medicaid, elder law planning, and taxation.

His LLM designation allows him to have a deeper understanding of tax implications, including estate taxes. Stephen's goal for all his clients is preserving their wealth and protecting their legacy—with a focus on tax mitigation and elimination and estate plans that meet his clients' every goal and need.

Stephen has taught thousands of attorneys and lay people by presenting continuing legal education lectures and public seminars on topics such as estate planning, probate proceedings, business and personal taxation, real estate taxation, business formation and planning, protection from scammers, trusts and wills, Medicaid asset protection, 1031 exchanges, and tax resolution strategies.

He can be reached at BonfaLawpc.com, where you can schedule a consultation directly on his online calendar.

To find Stephen Bonfa:

Website: https://www.ix-legal.com/
(where you can book a conversation with
him, watch an informational video, read his
newsletter, or sit back and just chill)

Instagram and TikTok: @Yourcasuallawyer

Facebook: https://www.facebook.com/
bonfalawpc/

YouTube: https://www.youtube.com/
@YourCasualLawyer

LinkedIn: https://www.linkedin.com/in/
stephen-bonfa-llm-7a9a65ab

Law Offices of
Stephen A Bonfa Esq PC
PRESERVING YOUR WEALTH; PROTECTING YOUR LEGACY